THE NEW SHARKS AND OCEAN LIFE ENCYCLOPEDIA

Claudia Martin

ARCTURUS

Picture Credits:
Key: b–bottom, t–top, c–center, l–left, r–right

Alamy Stock Photo: 6–7 (Norbert Probst/imageBROKER.com GmbH & Co. KG), 10–11 (Scenics and Science), 13t, 28–29, 47t (Paulo Oliveira), 14–15 (Andrey Nekrasov), 16–17, 246–247 (Helmut Corneli), 22–23 (Solvin Zankl/Nature Picture Library), 25t, 208b (SeaTops), 26t (PF-(usna1)), 28c (NC Collections), 30–31 (blickwinkel), 32–33 (Chris Gomersall), 36–37, 182c, 248–249 (David Fleetham), 40–41 (Georgette Apol/Steve Bloom Images), 44c (Norbert Wu/Minden Pictures), 44–45 (Solvin Zankl), 46–47 (World History Archive), 96–97 (Shaun Wilkinson), 106–107 (Christian Loader), 124br (Peter Horree), 138bc (Kelvin Aitken), 171t (Arco Images GmbH/G. Lacz), 174–175 (Michael Siluk), 180b (cbimages), 182b (WaterFrame), 188–189 (Masa Ushioda/Stephen Frink Collection), 190–191 (Tony Wu/Nature Picture Library), 194t (Pete Ryan/National Geographic Image Collection), 202b (blickwinkel/Frischknecht), 214–215 (Paul R. Sterry/Nature Photographers Ltd), 220c (FLPA), 220–221 (Richard Mittleman/Gon2Foto), 222b (David Tipling Photo Library), 224–225 (Rodrigo Friscione/Cultura Creative (RF)), 229b (Doug Allan/Nature Picture Library); **Blue Planet Archive:** 73no.7 (Makoto Kubo/e-Photo), 110–111, 110bc (Andy Murch), 111tr (D. R. Schrichte), 112–113 (Andre Seale), 112bl, 158–159 (Doug Perrine), 123bl (Toshio Minami/e-Photo), 126c, 127tc (Bruce Rasner), 132–133, 132bl (Makoto Hirose/e-Photo), 133c (David Shen), 134b (George W. Benz), 136b (Espen Rekdal), 137bl, 149tc (Jeff Rotman), 142–143 (Jeff Milisen), 143bc (Masa Ushioda), 146cr (John Muhilly), 150–151 (Saul Gonor), 150b, 151t (Marty Snyderman); **Bridgeman Images:** 159cr (Foundation for the Arts Collection, Anonymous Gift); **FLPA Images:** 18c (Mike Parry/Minden Pictures), 20b, 188b, 212c (Tui De Roy/Minden Pictures), 34l, 44b, 172c (Photo Researchers), 42–43, 192–193 (Flip Nicklin/Minden Pictures), 45t, 184cr, 184br (Norbert Wu/Minden Pictures), 170b (Steve Trewhella), 172–173 (Norbert Probst/Imagebroker), 194c (Hiroya Minakuchi/Minden Pictures), 194–195 (Peter Verhoog/Minden Pictures), 200c (Suzi Eszterhas/Minden Pictures), 200–201 (Frans Lanting), 201b (Kevin Schafer/Minden Pictures), 206–207 (Christophe Migeon/Biosphoto), 214c (Glenn Bartley, BIA/Minden Pictures), 226c (Jack Perks), 240c (Scott Leslie/Minden Pictures); **Getty Images:** 24–25 (Daniela Dirscherl), 98bc (Gerard Soury), 176–177 (Gerald Robert Fischer), 180–181 (marrio31), 182–183 (Rodrigo Friscione), 208–209 (Georgette Douwma), 218–219 (D Williams Photography), 240b (Mark Conlin), 244–245 (ullstein bild); **Istockphoto:** 135tl (Jedamus Lichtbilders); **Nature Picture Library:** 48–49, 52–53, 73no.8, 78–79, 78bc, 82–83, 88cl, 119c, 120br, 136–137, 140–141, 140c, 148–149, 148c, 152–153, 156–157, 157tl, 166b (Andy Murch), 54–55, 98–99, 131cr, 141tl, 146bc, 166–167 (Jeff Rotman), 54cr (Alex Hyde), 62–63 (Pete Oxford), 64–65 (Ralph Pace), 65cr, 118–119, 118bc, 120–121, 120cl, 130b, 144c (Doug Perrine), 66–67, 76–77 (Shane Gross), 80–81, 124cl, 138–139 (Jordi Chias), 114–115 (Chris & Monique Fallows), 116–117 (Richard Robinson), 124–125 (Sergio Hanquet), 126–127 (Bruce Rasner), 128–129, 128c, 129cr (Alex Mustard), 134–135 (Franco Banfi), 139tc, 145br (Solvin Zankl), 142bc (David Fleetham), 153br (Tony Wu), 160c (Luciano Candisani), 165tr (Jose B. Ruiz), 168–169 (Magnus Lundgren), 169bc (David Shale); **Science Photo Library:** 9t (Gary Hincks), 50c (DK Images), 56c (D & L Graphics), 155br (John Sibbick); **Shutterstock:** Cover (Popel Arseniy, Lucky Step, Arthur Balitskii, MoreVector, alyaBigJoy, Alexander_P, Marzufello, Rich Carey, bluehand, Vladimir Wrangel, Joe Dordo Brnobic, Jo Crebbin, Gudkov Andrey), 1c (Popel Arseniy), 1bl, 1r (Rich Carey), 1br (Lucky Step), 3tl, 20c (Collins93), 3tr, 72 (Sail Far Dive Deep), 3bl, 186br (Miroslav Halama), 4tl, 97bc (Richard Whitcombe), 4tr, 81tc (Becky Gill), 4bl, 94cr (Fata Morgana by Andrew Marriott), 5tl, 174bc, 174br, 186–187 (Cigdem Sean Cooper), 5tr, 202c, 216–217, 216b, 217t (Ondrej Prosicky), 5br, 211cr (Lorenzo Ragazzi), 6c (Marut Syannikroth), 6b (AshtonEa), 7t, 236b (SergeUWPhoto), 7b (Ian Dyball), 8c (Tea Oor), 9br (R McIntyre), 8–9 (titoOnz), 10cl (Dr. Norbert Lange), 10cc (Agami Photo Agency), 10cr (Craig Milson), 10bl (Gerald Robert Fischer), 10bc (Rattiya Phongdumhyu), 10br (Dmitry Reznichenko), 11tl (John A Anderson), 11tr (Ocean Image Photography), 12cr (Anna Filippenok), 12bl (Gena Melendrez), 12bc (Shane Gross), 12br (Joe Quinn), 12–13 (aquapix), 14cr (CK Ma), 14cl (Oksana Maksymova), 14b (painapple), 15t (feathercollector), 16cr (Grobler du Preez), 16bl (Joanne Weston), 16bc (Jeff Stamer), 16br, 233b, 234–235 (zaferkizilkaya), 17b (Chase Dekker), 18b (Tomas Kotouc), 18–19 (Jack Pokoj), 19b (Stephanie Rousseau), 20–21 (Andrew Astbury), 21b (Roger Clark ARPS), 22c, 28b (NoPainNoGain), 22b, 189t, 191b (wildestanimal), 23b, 204c, 206b (Tarpan), 24c (Ethan Daniels), 24b, 38b, 40b (Rich Carey), 26c, 175t (Dennis Jacobsen), 26b (Zaruba Ondrej), 26–27 (Gabriel Guzman), 27b (LouisLotterPhotography), 29t (Aleksander Karpenko), 30c (Paul A Carpenter), 30b (Bildagentur Zoonar GmbH), 31t (Gerald Marella), 32cl (Nigel Wallace), 32cr (FredChan), 32b (Cary Kalscheuer), 33tr (pzAxe), 34b (aDam Wildlife), 34–35, 244b, 249t (Damsea), 35b (wonderisland), 36c (Gilberto Villasana), 36b (steve estvanik), 37b (NatureDiver), 38c, 39t, 196c (Laura Dinraths), 38–39 (David John Ciavarella), 41c (fenkieandreas), 41b (Vladimir Wrangel), 42c (reisegraf.ch), 43t (Rudmer Zwerver), 49br (Stefan Pircher), 48b, 58br, 60–61, 66c, 67cr, 73no.5, 144–145 (wildestanimal), 49tl (Illia Khurtin), 50–51 (Damsea), 50b, 104cr (slowmotiongli), 51tl, 52c (kaschibo), 52br, 53tc (Alessandro De Maddalena), 54bl (Nazir Amin), 55tr (Dotted Yeti), 56–57 (Pavaphon Supanantananont), 56br, 73no.4 (Boris Pamikov), 57bl, 82bc, 83tr (Martin Voeller), 59, 59tr, 66br, 29cr, 75tl, 122–123 (Tomas Kotouc), 58cl, 63tr (Fiona Ayerst), 58br, 130–131 (HikeAndShoot), 60c (EreborMountain), 61tc (Natalie11345), 61br, 76cr (FtLaud), 62bc, 74–75 (Richard Condlyffe), 63bl, 116cr (Martin Prochazcacz), 64c (Matthias Jiury Rabbione), 64br (Michael_19), 68–69 (Herschel Hoffmeyer), 68c (Marcel Clemens), 69br (Michael Rosskothen), 70–71 (Martin_Hristov), 70bl (Maridav), 71tr (Allen Haggerty), 71br (sirtravelalot), 73no.1 (Matt9122), 73no.2 (Beat J Korner), 73no.3 (Ramon Carretero), 73no.6 (Captain_Dnl), 74cl (Joe Dordo Brnobic), 77c, 104bl (Vladimir Wrangel), 79c (Madelein Wolfaardt), 80c (Pinosub), 84–85 (Maui Topical Images), 84bl (timsimages.uk), 86–87, 100bl (Yann hubert), 86c (frantisekhojdysz), 87bc (Anita Kainrath), 88–89 (Carlos Grillo), 89tc (Ciurzynski), 90–91 (Love Lego), 90c, 91tr (Matt9122), 92–93 (Ciril Monteiro), 92cl (Dudarev Mikhail), 93br (icemanphotos), 94–95 (Onusa Putapitak), 95tc (David Evison), 96c (John Back), 98cl (Dirk van der Heide), 100–101 (Keith Levit), 100cr (Izen Kai), 102–103 (IanRedding), 102cl (Tum3000), 103tr (Charlotte Bleijenberg), 104–105 (Gabriel Guzman), 106cr (Johan Larson), 107bc (Ethan Daniels), 108–109 (Jemma Craig), 108c (Daniel Lamborn), 109tr (Teguh Tirtaputra), 112cr (Roser Gari Perez), 114c (Sergey Uryadnikov), 115tl (Jsegalexplore), 117tc (Lukas Walter), 122cl (HunterKitty), 146–147 (Joe Belanger), 152cl (Valda Butterworth), 154–155 (Rich Carey), 154cr (Catmando), 156b (saiko3p), 158bc (Andrea Izzotti), 160–161, 161tr (Arunee Rodloy), 162–163 (Gudkov Andrey), 162c (Krzysztof Odziomek), 163cr (Divefriday), 164–165 (Maya Parl), 164c (stephan kerkhofs), 167tl (Khairil Azhar Junos), 168br (Greg Amptman), 170c (Tropical studio), 170–171 (scubaluna), 172bc (Gerald Robert Fischer), 173c (Michael Warwick), 174c (Alex_Vinci), 176c (divedog), 176b (Silk-stocking), 177b (ligio), 178c (yaodiving), 178bc (Kichigin), 178br (NaniP), 178–179 (besjunior), 179t, 181t, 248c (orlandin), 180c (Anne Frijling), 183b (lunamarina), 184–185 (Jack Potoj), 185tr (divelvanov), 186cl and cr (Jesus Cobaleda), 187t (DiveSpin.Com), 188c (Jo Crebbin), 190c, 193b (Andrea Izzotti), 190b (John Wollwerth), 192c (Tory Kallman), 192b (Andrew Sutton), 196b (Liquid Productions, LLC), 196–197 (Greg Amptman), 197b (Jiri Prochazka), 198c (AndreAnita), 198b (Alexey Seafarer), 198–199 (FloridaStock), 199b (Caleb Foster), 200b (Chanonry), 202–203 (Hal Brindley), 203b (Pascal Halder), 204b (David Osborn), 204–205 (Pat Stornebrink), 205b (Nicram Sabod), 206c (Wonderly Imaging), 207b (Philip Bird LRPS CPAGB), 208c (shakeelmsm), 209t (William Healy Photography), 210–211 (Lauren Suryanata), 210c (Ery Azmeer), 210b (Elements_Brisbane), 212–213, 225b (Don Mammoser), 212br (Henri Leduc), 213c (Angela N Perryman), 214b (anirbandas08081986), 215c (John L. Absher), 216c (Nolleks86), 218b (Bernie Van Der Vyver), 219cc (Karel Gallas), 219tr (Wolf Avni), 219b (Dennis Von Linden), 220b, 244c (Brian Lasenby), 221b (Frank Fichtmueller), 222–223 (Jeremy Richards), 223t (jaroslava V), 224c (Ray Hennessy), 224b (RHIMAGE), 226bc (Erni), 226br (Brian E Kushner), 226–227 (Simonas Minkevicius), 227b (Rob Francis), 228c, 228b (Nick Pecker), 228–229 (Enrique Aguirre), 230–231, 248b (Brandon B), 230c (ChameleonsEye), 230b (MZPHOTO.CZ), 231b (Lynsey Allan), 232c, 246c (Richard Whitcombe), 232–233, 250c, 251bl (blue-sea.cz), 234c (Martin Prochazkacz), 235b (Kondratuk Aleksei), 235bl (Tignogartnahc), 236c (subphoto), 236–237 (Yusran Abdul Rahman), 237t (Evan Hallein), 238c (Jay Gao), 238b (Petr Malyshev), 238–239 (Uwe Bergwitz), 239t (Jarib), 240–241 (Levent Konuk), 241t (RLS Photo), 242c (AlessandroZocc), 242b (Vladyslav Danilin), 242–243 (Bill45), 243t (Arunee Rodloy), 245b (Joe Belanger), 246b (Eugene Kalenkovich), 247t (Mark Willian Kirkland), 250b (Leo Lorenzo), 250–251 (Levent Albas); **Wikimedia Commons:** 42b (Uwe Kils), 46t (MARUM – Zentrum für Marine Umweltwissenschaften, Universität Bremen), 46b (NOAA Okeanos Explorer Program, Galapagos Rift Expedition 2011), 232b (Aquapix and Expedition to the Deep Slope 2007, NOAA-OE), 194b (Paula Olson, NOAA), 195t (GregTheBusker).

This edition published in 2024 by Arcturus Publishing Limited
26/27 Bickels Yard, 151–153 Bermondsey Street,
London SE1 3HA

Copyright © Arcturus Holdings Limited

All rights reserved. No part of this publication may be reproduced, stored in a retrieval system, or transmitted, in any form or by any means, electronic, mechanical, photocopying, recording or otherwise, without prior written permission in accordance with the provisions of the Copyright Act 1956 (as amended). Any person or persons who do any unauthorised act in relation to this publication may be liable to criminal prosecution and civil claims for damages.

ISBN: 978-1-3988-4860-3
CH012466US
Supplier 29, Date 0724, PI 00007979

Author and Editor: Claudia Martin
Editor: Lydia Halliday
Designers: Lorraine Inglis and Amy McSimpson
Consultant: Jules Howard
Managing Designer: Rosie Bellwood-Moyler
Managing Editor: Joe Harris

Printed in China

A note on large numbers:

1 million	1,000,000
1 billion	1,000,000,000
1 trillion	1,000,000,000,000
1 quadrillion	1,000,000,000,000,000
1 quintillion	1,000,000,000,000,000,000
1 sextillion	1,000,000,000,000,000,000,000
1 septillion	1,000,000,000,000,000,000,000,000

Contents

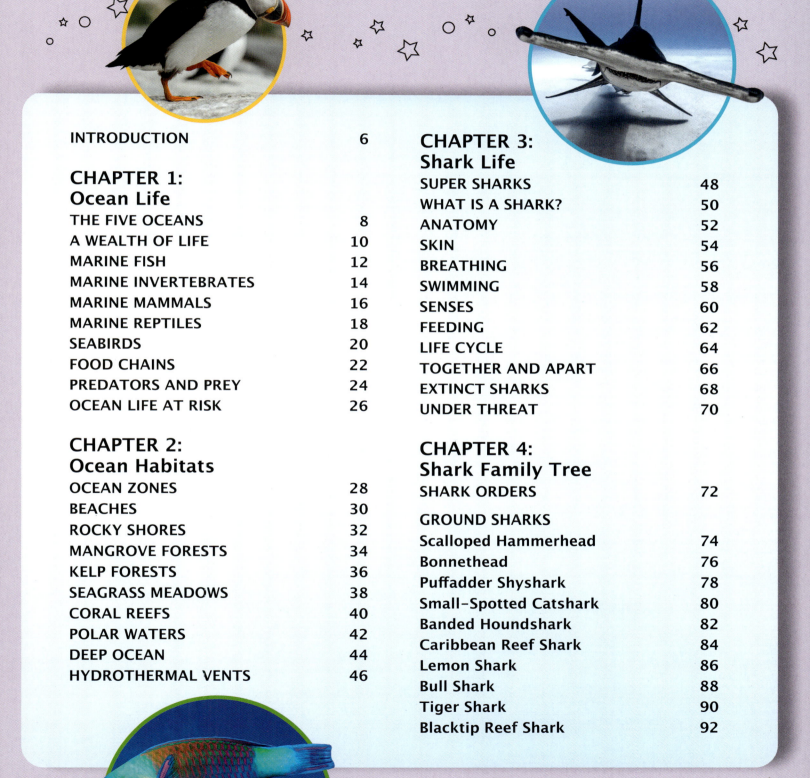

INTRODUCTION	6

CHAPTER 1:
Ocean Life

THE FIVE OCEANS	8
A WEALTH OF LIFE	10
MARINE FISH	12
MARINE INVERTEBRATES	14
MARINE MAMMALS	16
MARINE REPTILES	18
SEABIRDS	20
FOOD CHAINS	22
PREDATORS AND PREY	24
OCEAN LIFE AT RISK	26

CHAPTER 2:
Ocean Habitats

OCEAN ZONES	28
BEACHES	30
ROCKY SHORES	32
MANGROVE FORESTS	34
KELP FORESTS	36
SEAGRASS MEADOWS	38
CORAL REEFS	40
POLAR WATERS	42
DEEP OCEAN	44
HYDROTHERMAL VENTS	46

CHAPTER 3:
Shark Life

SUPER SHARKS	48
WHAT IS A SHARK?	50
ANATOMY	52
SKIN	54
BREATHING	56
SWIMMING	58
SENSES	60
FEEDING	62
LIFE CYCLE	64
TOGETHER AND APART	66
EXTINCT SHARKS	68
UNDER THREAT	70

CHAPTER 4:
Shark Family Tree

SHARK ORDERS	72

GROUND SHARKS

Scalloped Hammerhead	74
Bonnethead	76
Puffadder Shyshark	78
Small-Spotted Catshark	80
Banded Houndshark	82
Caribbean Reef Shark	84
Lemon Shark	86
Bull Shark	88
Tiger Shark	90
Blacktip Reef Shark	92

CARPET SHARKS
Whale Shark	94
Zebra Shark	96
Blind Shark	98
Nurse Shark	100
Brownbanded Bamboo Shark	102
Epaulette Shark	104
Indonesian Speckled Shark	106
Tasselled Wobbegong	108
Ornate Wobbegong	110
Necklace Carpet Shark	112

MACKEREL SHARKS
Great White Shark	114
Shortfin Mako Shark	116
Porbeagle	118
Salmon Shark	120
Sand Tiger Shark	122
Smalltooth Sand Tiger Shark	124
Megamouth Shark	126
Basking Shark	128
Pelagic Thresher	130
Goblin Shark	132

DOGFISH SHARKS
Greenland Shark	134
Velvet Belly Lanternshark	136
Angular Roughshark	138
Spiny Dogfish	140
Cookiecutter Shark	142

FRILLED AND COW SHARKS
Broadnose Sevengill Shark	144

BULLHEAD SHARKS
Horn Shark	146
Japanese Bullhead Shark	148

SAWSHARKS
Longnose Sawshark	150

ANGELSHARKS
Japanese Angelshark	152

CHAPTER 5:
Other Cartilaginous Fish
CARTILAGINOUS EVOLUTION	154
GUITARFISH	156
SAWFISH	158
RIVER STINGRAYS	160
MOBULA RAYS	162
ELECTRIC RAYS	164
SKATES	166
CHIMAERAS	168

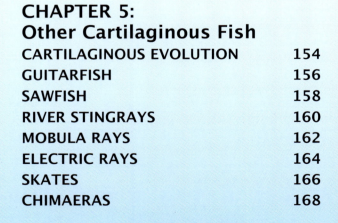

CHAPTER 6: Bony Fish
FLATFISH	170
SEAHORSES	172
BOXFISH AND RELATIVES	174
SURGEONFISH AND RELATIVES	176
SCORPIONFISH	178
DRAGONETS	180
BILLFISH	182
ANGLERFISH	184
PARROTFISH	186

CHAPTER 7: Mammals
BALEEN WHALES	188
TOOTHED WHALES	190
DOLPHINS	192
PORPOISES	194
SEA COWS	196
POLAR BEAR	198
OTTERS	200
WALRUS	202
SEALS	204
EARED SEALS	206

CHAPTER 8: Reptiles
SEA TURTLES	208
SEA CROCODILES	210
MARINE IGUANA	212

CHAPTER 9: Birds
PLOVERS AND RELATIVES	214
FLAMINGOS	216
HERONS AND RELATIVES	218
LARIDS	220
TUBENOSES	222
GANNETS AND RELATIVES	224
SEA DUCKS	226
PUFFINS AND RELATIVES	228
PENGUINS	230

CHAPTER 10: Invertebrates
ANTHOZOA	232
JELLYFISH	234
OCTOPUS AND SQUID	236
CRABS	238
LOBSTERS AND RELATIVES	240
BIVALVES	242
SEA SLUGS AND SNAILS	244
STARFISH	246
SEA CUCUMBERS AND URCHINS	248
WORMS	250

GLOSSARY	252
INDEX	255

Introduction

The oceans are so wide and deep that they provide 90 percent of all the living space on Earth. Their water offers food, transport, shelter—and life—to trillions of living things, from sawsharks that rest on the seafloor to gulls that soar high above the waves.

Many Habitats

From wave-washed beaches to the dark ocean floor, from coral reefs to polar ice, there are many different ocean habitats. Some habitats offer shelter for animals, such as soft sand for tunneling or seagrass for hiding. Every habitat offers food for its inhabitants, whether that is sardines to snap up or seaweed to graze on.

The Galápagos shark is a ground shark, a group of sharks with wide, sharp-toothed mouths.

This mangrove crab hides from predators by burrowing into wet mud along the shore. It surfaces to hunt for plants and small animals to eat.

Up to 3 m (9.8 ft) long, this shark feeds on fish, octopus, fur seals, sea lions, and marine iguanas.

Different Bodies

The bodies of ocean animals are well suited to their habitat. Many deep-sea fish have large eyes for seeing in dim waters, while penguins have a thick layer of fat for warmth in freezing seas. Studying each animal's body can also reveal its method of travel—or that it does not travel at all. Mackerel sharks have a sleek body for swimming fast in the open ocean. Tube worms root themselves to the ocean floor, pulling inside their tough tube for safety.

Sea spiders are not closely related to land spiders, although they walk in a similar way on their eight legs. They can also swim over the seafloor by waving their legs.

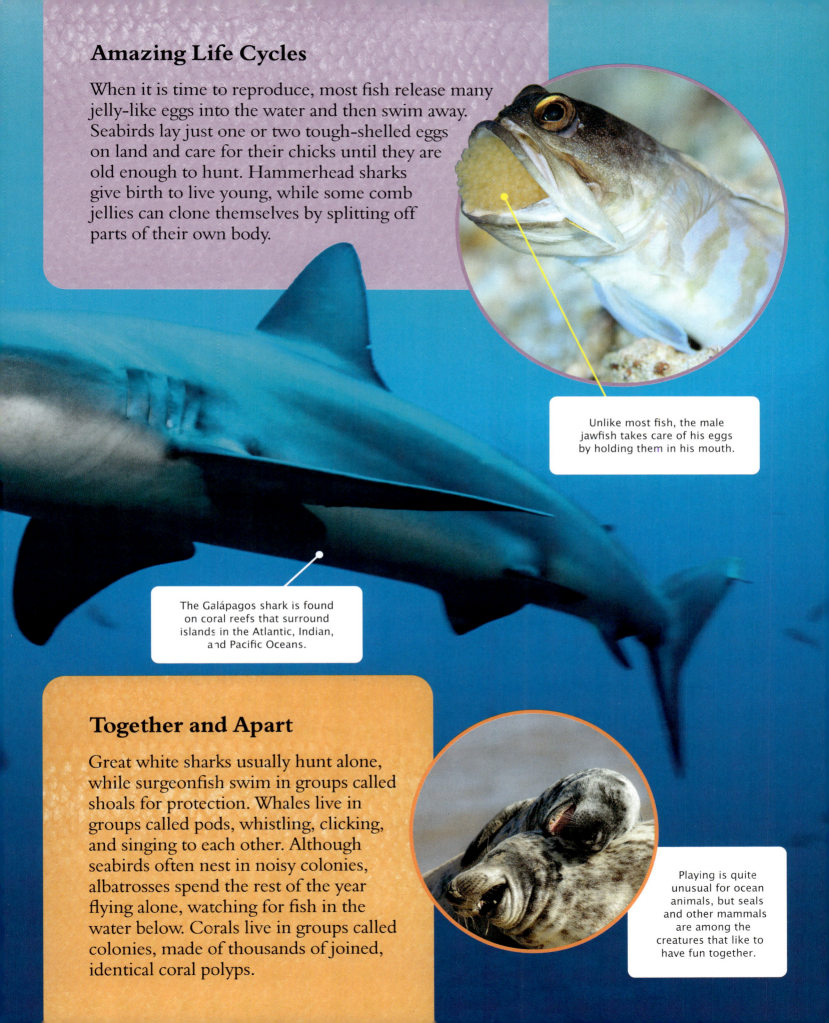

Amazing Life Cycles

When it is time to reproduce, most fish release many jelly-like eggs into the water and then swim away. Seabirds lay just one or two tough-shelled eggs on land and care for their chicks until they are old enough to hunt. Hammerhead sharks give birth to live young, while some comb jellies can clone themselves by splitting off parts of their own body.

Unlike most fish, the male jawfish takes care of his eggs by holding them in his mouth.

The Galápagos shark is found on coral reefs that surround islands in the Atlantic, Indian, and Pacific Oceans.

Together and Apart

Great white sharks usually hunt alone, while surgeonfish swim in groups called shoals for protection. Whales live in groups called pods, whistling, clicking, and singing to each other. Although seabirds often nest in noisy colonies, albatrosses spend the rest of the year flying alone, watching for fish in the water below. Corals live in groups called colonies, made of thousands of joined, identical coral polyps.

Playing is quite unusual for ocean animals, but seals and other mammals are among the creatures that like to have fun together.

Chapter 1: Ocean Life
The Five Oceans

Water covers more than two-thirds of our planet's surface. Nearly 97 percent of this water is saltwater, with just 3 percent made up of freshwater in rivers, ponds, and lakes. Saltwater fills a vast world ocean, which humans have named as five oceans.

Salty Water

The ocean tastes salty because it contains particles of sodium and chloride. Together, these make sodium chloride, which is better known as table salt. These particles, and other minerals, arrived in the ocean through a process called weathering. As rain falls, it collects carbon dioxide from the air. This gas mixes with the water to make carbonic acid. Acids can wear away materials, so as rainwater runs over rocks, it carries away tiny particles, including sodium and chloride. Rivers and streams carry the particles to the ocean.

The **Pacific Ocean** is both the largest and deepest ocean, with an average depth of 4,000 m (13,000 ft).

The **Arctic Ocean** is almost completely covered by ice in winter.

In Pattani, Thailand, salt is gathered on the beach. When the seawater evaporates, or turns to gas, in the hot sun, it leaves behind the solid salt.

AREAS OF THE OCEANS

Pacific Ocean: 168,723,000 sq km (65,144,000 sq miles)
Atlantic Ocean: 85,133,000 sq km (32,870,000 sq miles)
Indian Ocean: 70,560,000 sq km (27,243,000 sq miles)
Southern Ocean: 21,960,000 sq km (8,479,000 sq miles)
Arctic Ocean: 15,558,000 sq km (6,007,000 sq miles)

Islands of the Maldives, in the Indian Ocean

DID YOU KNOW? If all the salt in the ocean was spread across Earth's land, it would form a layer more than 150 m (500 ft) thick.

Moving Water

Ocean water is constantly moving. As the wind blows across the surface, it whips up waves, which travel right across the ocean until they curl over and "break" on the shore. Currents are great rivers of water that snake around the oceans. Some currents are caused by wind, while others are caused by differences in water temperature. At the surface or closer to the equator, the water is warmer. Warm water rises, while cold water sinks, setting off global movements.

Major currents flow clockwise in the northern hemisphere and anticlockwise in the southern hemisphere. These directions are caused by the turning of the planet, which shifts water and winds to the right north of the equator, but the opposite way south of the equator.

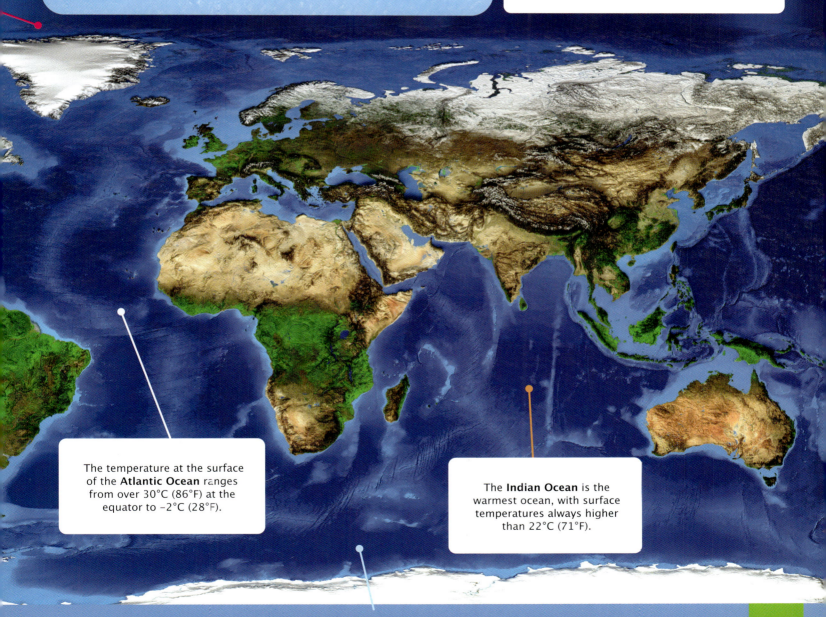

The temperature at the surface of the **Atlantic Ocean** ranges from over 30°C (86°F) at the equator to −2°C (28°F).

The **Indian Ocean** is the warmest ocean, with surface temperatures always higher than 22°C (71°F).

The **Southern Ocean** surrounds the continent of Antarctica.

A Wealth of Life

Around 4 billion years ago, the first living things formed in the oceans. They were microorganisms, too small to be seen by the human eye. Today, microorganisms make up 70 percent of the weight of all the ocean's living things. Larger life forms include animals, plants, and fungi.

Kingdoms

Scientists often divide living things into "kingdoms," based on characteristics such as the number and type of cells from which they are made. Cells are the building blocks for all living things. All the kingdoms include "marine" forms, which live in or around the ocean.

KINGDOM: Bacteria and archaea
CELLS: One simple cell
CHARACTERISTICS: Reproduce by splitting into parts
LENGTH: 0.00015 to 0.015 mm (0.000006 to 0.0006 in)

Cyanobacteria under a microscope

KINGDOM: Plants
CELLS: Many types of complex cells
CHARACTERISTICS: Make their own food from sunlight and cannot move
LENGTH: 0.002 mm to 115 m (0.00008 in to 377 ft)

Glasswort

KINGDOM: Fungi
CELLS: One or many complex cells
CHARACTERISTICS: Must absorb food and cannot move
LENGTH: 0.005 mm to 3 km (0.0002 in to 9,800 ft)

Lichen, formed when fungi and cyanobacteria live together

KINGDOM: Animals
CELLS: Many types of complex cells
CHARACTERISTICS: Breathe oxygen, cannot make their own food, and can move
LENGTH: 0.008 mm to 37 m (0.0003 in to 120 ft)

Peacock mantis shrimp

KINGDOM: Protozoa
CELLS: One complex cell
CHARACTERISTICS: Cannot make their own food and usually able to move
LENGTH: 0.001 mm to 20 cm (0.00004 to 4 in)

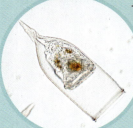

Tintinnid under a microscope

KINGDOM: Chromists
CELLS: One or many complex cells
CHARACTERISTICS: Make their own food from sunlight
LENGTH: 0.001 mm to 45 m (0.00004 in to 150 ft)

Fucus algae

DID YOU KNOW? Around 250,000 marine species have been named, but scientists think there are at least 750,000 more to be found.

Species

A species, such as the great hammerhead shark, is a group of living things that can mate with one another and produce healthy babies. Scientists arrange species into bigger groups, such as genus, order, class, and kingdom, based on their similarities. The great hammerhead is in the genus of hammerhead sharks, in the order of ground sharks, in the class of cartilaginous fish, in the kingdom of animals.

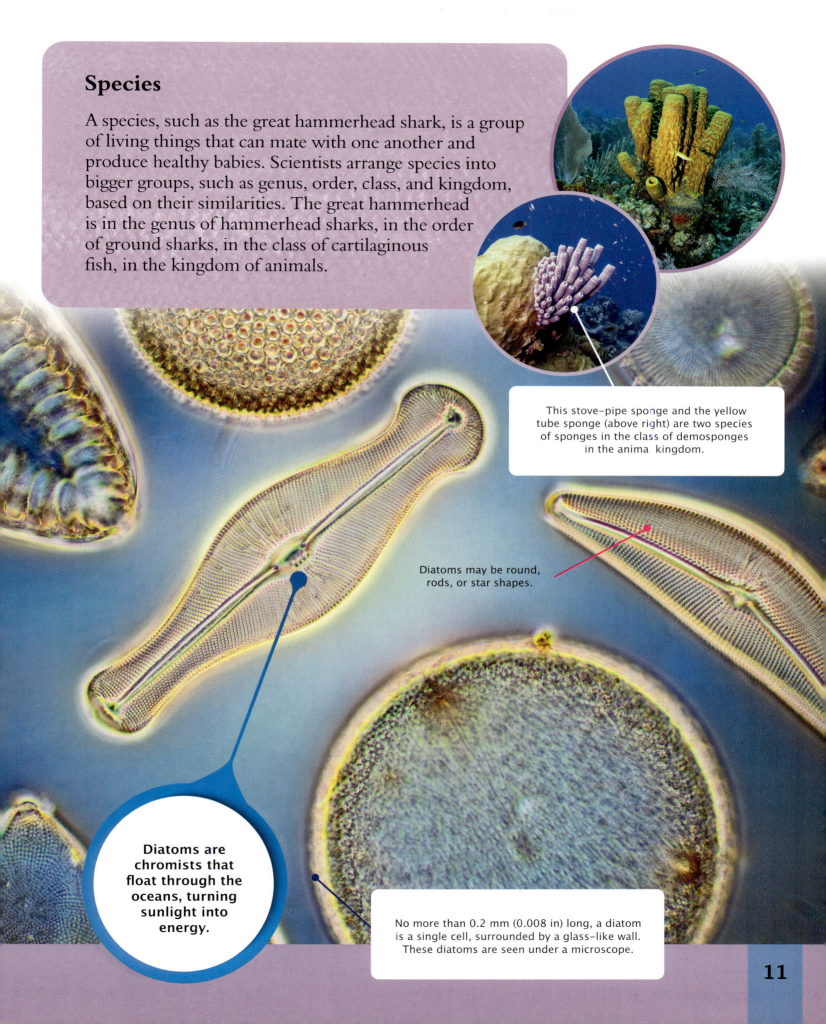

This stove-pipe sponge and the yellow tube sponge (above right) are two species of sponges in the class of demosponges in the animal kingdom.

Diatoms may be round, rods, or star shapes.

Diatoms are chromists that float through the oceans, turning sunlight into energy.

No more than 0.2 mm (0.008 in) long, a diatom is a single cell, surrounded by a glass-like wall. These diatoms are seen under a microscope.

Marine Fish

At least 16,000 species of fish live in the ocean. Fish breathe by taking oxygen from the water using their gills. Most fish swim by waving their body or tail, while steering with their fins. Many fish, but not all of them, have skin covered in hard plates called scales.

Breathing through Gills

Fish breathe by gulping water into their mouth. Water contains lots of oxygen. The water flows through the gills, which are filled with tiny blood vessels. The blood vessels soak up the oxygen, which the fish's heart pumps round the body. The used water is released through the gill slits.

Fish Features

KEY
1. GILLS
2. HEART
3. PELVIC FIN
4. STOMACH
5. ANAL FIN
6. CAUDAL FIN
7. DORSAL FINS

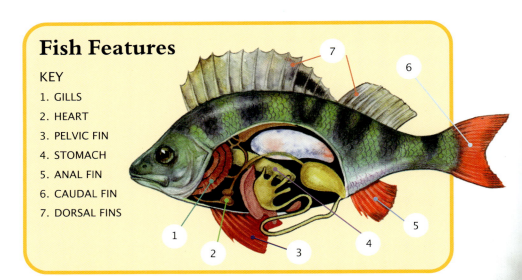

Classes of Fish

There are three classes of fish, which have different body features. The earliest fish to evolve were jawless fish, but most of them are now extinct.

JAWLESS FISH

CHARACTERISTICS: These fish have no jaws for biting, so they feed by sucking. They have long, scale-less bodies.

SPECIES: Hagfish and lampreys

A lamprey mouth

CARTILAGINOUS FISH

CHARACTERISTICS: This class of jawed fish have a skeleton made of bendy cartilage. Their skin has many tooth-like scales.

SPECIES: Sharks, skates, and rays

Thresher shark

BONY FISH

CHARACTERISTICS: These jawed fish have skeletons made of bone. Their scales are usually smooth and overlapping.

SPECIES: All other fish

Yellowtail snapper

MARINE FISH RECORDS

Heaviest and longest: Whale shark, up to 21,300 kg (47,000 lb) and 12.65 m (41.5 ft) long
Longest bony fish: Giant oarfish, up to 11 m (36 ft)
Shortest: Male *Photocorynus spiniceps* anglerfish, as small as 6.2 mm (0.24 in)
Fastest swimmer: Black marlin, up to 105 km/h (65 mph)
Longest living: Greenland shark, possibly up to 400 years

Giant oarfish

Like in other bony fish, the gill slit is protected by a hard cover called the operculum.

The squirrelfish is nocturnal, or active at night. It has large eyes so it can gather as much light as possible.

Pectoral fins, on either side of the head, help with steering.

DID YOU KNOW? Female sunfish produce more eggs than any other fish, releasing up to 300 million of them into the water.

13

Marine Invertebrates

> With its squidgy, jelly-like body, the warty comb jelly is in the ctenophore phylum.

Around 580 to 550 million years ago, the first animals moved in the oceans. These early animals were all invertebrates. Invertebrates are animals that do not have a backbone—or any other bones inside their body. Apart from that, invertebrates can be very different from each other.

Many Different Bodies

Scientists divide invertebrates into 30 different groups, called phylums, based on their body plan. In contrast, all animals with a backbone—fish, mammals, reptiles, amphibians, and birds—are in just one phylum. Some invertebrates, such as nematode worms, are completely soft-bodied. Others, called arthropods, have an exoskeleton, or hard covering, to protect their boneless body. Marine arthropods include crabs and lobsters. Other invertebrates, called molluscs, have a muscly covering called a mantle. In some molluscs, such as snails and clams, the mantle builds a hard shell.

Members of the chordate phylum, sea squirts are tube-shaped animals that attach to rocks. They feed by sucking in water and tiny creatures.

The tiger egg cowry is a species of sea snail in the mollusc phylum.

Looking at Fossils

Fossils are the preserved remains of ancient living things. Scientists study fossils to find out how animals have evolved, or changed over time, and when different groups of animals first appeared. The oldest invertebrate fossils are of simple sponges.

This is fossilized brain coral, which is in the cnidarian phylum.

14

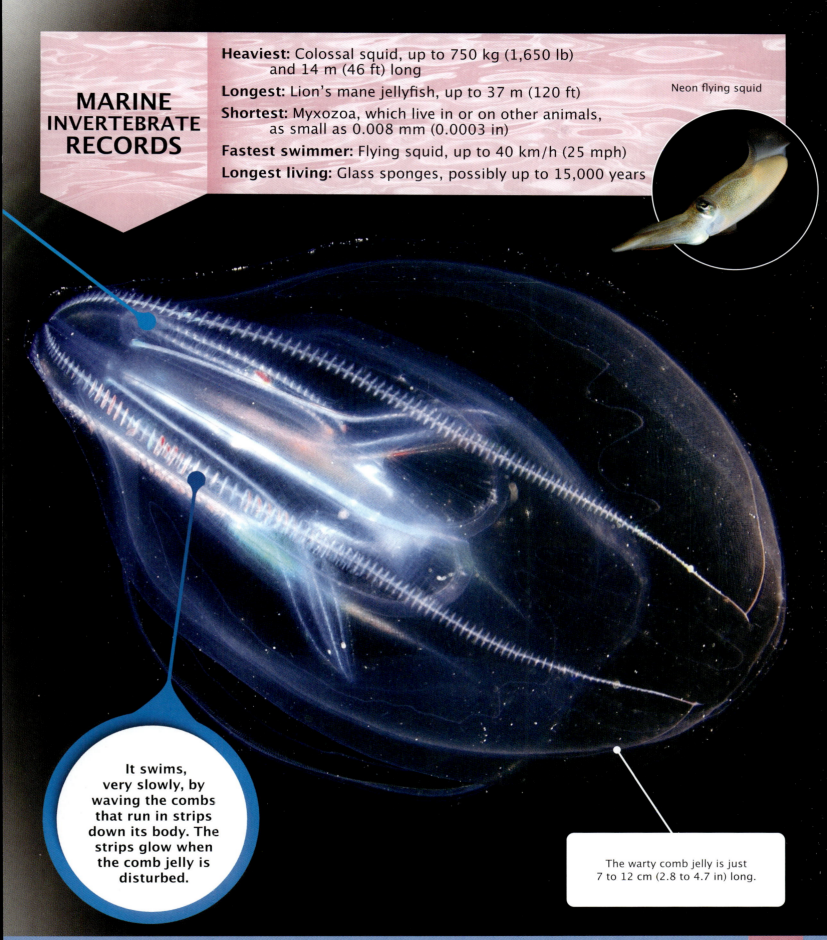

MARINE INVERTEBRATE RECORDS

Heaviest: Colossal squid, up to 750 kg (1,650 lb) and 14 m (46 ft) long
Longest: Lion's mane jellyfish, up to 37 m (120 ft)
Shortest: Myxozoa, which live in or on other animals, as small as 0.008 mm (0.0003 in)
Fastest swimmer: Flying squid, up to 40 km/h (25 mph)
Longest living: Glass sponges, possibly up to 15,000 years

Neon flying squid

It swims, very slowly, by waving the combs that run in strips down its body. The strips glow when the comb jelly is disturbed.

The warty comb jelly is just 7 to 12 cm (2.8 to 4.7 in) long.

DID YOU KNOW? Invertebrates make up 96 percent of all the species of animals living in and around the world's oceans.

15

Marine Mammals

Around 126 species of mammals spend all or part of their life in the ocean. Like other mammals—including humans—these animals need to breathe air, so they come to the water surface regularly. All female mammals feed their young on milk.

Family Life

All marine mammals give birth to live young. Apart from polar bears, which have up to three cubs, marine mammals have just one baby at a time, which they look after for several months or even years. All marine mammals make sounds to communicate with each other, from the songs of whales to the barks of seals.

A Cape fur seal feeds her pup on milk for the first six months.

Groups of Marine Mammals

Marine mammals are not all closely related to each other: they belong to different scientific groups with quite different bodies and lifestyles.

CETACEANS

CHARACTERISTICS: These mammals never leave the water. They have a streamlined body and two limbs that are flippers.

SPECIES: Around 85 whales, dolphins, and porpoises

SEA COWS

CHARACTERISTICS: Sea cows never leave the water. They have a rounded body and two limbs that are flippers

SPECIES: 3 manatees and a dugong

CARNIVORANS

CHARACTERISTICS: These clawed meat-eaters spend part of their life on land. They have four limbs, which are flipper-like in sea lions, seals, and walruses

SPECIES: 38 sea lions, walruses, seals, otters, and polar bears

Minke whale

West Indian manatee

Mediterranean monk seal

Atlantic spotted dolphins develop their spots only as they grow older. This mother is fully spotted.

These dolphins communicate with squawks, whistles, and buzzes.

This young dolphin, called a calf, is gray-white, with no spots at all. It will be cared for by its mother for up to five years.

Blue whale

MARINE MAMMAL RECORDS

Heaviest and longest: Blue whale, up to 173,000 kg (381,000 lb) and 33.6 m (110 ft) long

Heaviest and longest carnivoran: Southern elephant seal, up to 5,000 kg (11,000 lb) and 6.8 m (22.5 ft) long

Shortest: Marine otter, as small as 87 cm (34 in) long

Fastest swimmer: Common dolphin, up to 64 km/h (40 mph)

Longest living: Bowhead whale, possibly up to 200 years

DID YOU KNOW? All mammals grow hair at some point in their life, but whales and dolphins are completely or nearly hairless as adults.

Marine Reptiles

The first reptiles lived on land, but around 299 to 252 million years ago, some reptiles adapted to life in the ocean. Today, there are around 12,000 species of reptiles, but only about 80 are marine. Reptiles need to breathe air into their lungs, so they come to the surface regularly.

Groups of Marine Reptiles

Marine reptiles belong to three orders. The turtle order contains 7 species of sea turtles. The crocodilian order contains 2 species of crocodiles that swim in the ocean. The squamate order contains 1 species of marine iguana and around 69 species of sea snakes. Squamates have skin protected by small, overlapping scales. Turtles and crocodiles grow harder bony plates called scutes.

Like most reptiles, a saltwater crocodile lays tough-shelled eggs on land. To break out of its shell, the baby uses a horny piece of skin on the tip of its snout called an egg-tooth.

Sea Snakes

Of all marine reptiles, sea snakes are best adapted to life in the ocean. While most marine reptiles have to go ashore to lay eggs and perhaps to rest, the majority of sea snakes never leave the ocean. They even give birth to live, swimming young in the water. Only the sea snakes known as kraits go on land to lay eggs.

It kills eels and other fish by biting with its sharp fangs, which inject a dose of venom.

With its paddle-like tail, the ornate sea snake is an excellent swimmer. Although it must surface eventually to breathe, it can absorb some oxygen from the water through its skin.

DID YOU KNOW? The sea snake with the deadliest venom is the Dubois' sea snake, but luckily it does not inject enough venom to kill a human with a single bite.

The yellow-lipped sea krait returns to land to rest, digest its food, and lay eggs.

This sea krait grows to 1.42 m (4.7 ft) long.

A newly hatched leatherback sea turtle makes its way to the sea.

MARINE REPTILE RECORDS

Heaviest and longest: Saltwater crocodile, up to 1,360 kg (3,000 lb) and 6.3 m (20.7 ft) long

Heaviest and longest turtle: Leatherback sea turtle, up to 650 kg (1,430 lb) and 2.1 m (7 ft) long

Shortest: Marine iguana, as small as 29 cm (11.4 in) long

Fastest swimmer: Leatherback sea turtle, up to 35 km/h (21 mph)

Longest living: Saltwater crocodile, possibly more than 100 years

Seabirds

Around 170 million years ago, birds started to evolve from reptiles called dinosaurs. Like most reptiles, birds lay hard-shelled eggs on land. All birds have wings, a beak, and a covering of feathers. Seabirds find their food beaneath the waves, on the ocean surface, or at the shoreline.

Adapted to the Sea

Seabirds have features that help them survive in and around the ocean. Since too much salt is dangerous for birds, many seabirds have glands in their head to remove the salt they swallow while drinking and eating. Seabird wings may be flipper-like for swimming beneath the surface, or extra-wide for flying great distances over the oceans in search of food. Many seabirds have webbed feet, with skin and tissue joining the toes, making them paddle-like for swimming.

The Atlantic puffin dives as deep as 68 m (223 ft) in search of fish. It uses its short, flipper-like wings as paddles, while steering with its webbed feet.

Careful Parents

Seabirds lay fewer eggs than most other birds, many laying just one egg per year. They also spend longer caring for their chicks, with frigatebirds giving the most time—14 months. Seabirds need a different strategy from landbirds because parenting by the stormy sea is dangerous and exhausting, as parents often travel far in search of food for their chicks. By putting all their energy into fewer chicks, hopefully one will survive.

Blue-footed boobies often have two chicks, but the eggs hatch four or five days apart, so the parents do not have two helpless newborns to care for at once.

The white-tailed sea eagle has the largest wingspan (from wingtip to wingtip) of any eagle, reaching 2.45 m (8 ft). It lives around ocean coasts as well as lakes and rivers.

Like other eagles, this bird has a hooked beak for ripping into its prey.

It uses its sharp claws to snatch fish from near the water surface, usually getting only its feet wet.

Emperor penguins

SEABIRD RECORDS

Heaviest: Emperor penguin, up to 45 kg (100 lb) and 1.3 m (4.3 ft) tall
Largest wingspan: Wandering albatross, up to 3.7 m (12.1 ft) wide
Shortest: Least storm petrel, as small as 13 cm (5.1 in) long
Fastest swimmer: Gentoo penguin, up to 36 km/h (22 mph)
Longest living: Laysan albatross, possibly more than 66 years

DID YOU KNOW? An Arctic tern flies around 2.4 million km (1.5 million miles) in its life, between Arctic coasts in the northern summer and Antarctica in the southern summer.

Food Chains

A food chain is a series of living things that are linked to each other because each feeds on the next in the series. At the top of a food chain is an apex predator, or "top hunter," an animal so big and fierce that it is not usually hunted by anything else.

Making Energy

At the bottom of ocean food chains are the living things that make their own food by turning sunlight into food energy through a process called photosynthesis. These living things are called producers. Many of them are microorganisms such as cyanobacteria, diatoms, and tiny plants. These microorganisms usually cannot move, so they float along near the sunlit water surface. They are called phytoplankton, from the ancient Greek for "plant drifter." Larger producers include plants, such as seagrass, and chromists, such as algae.

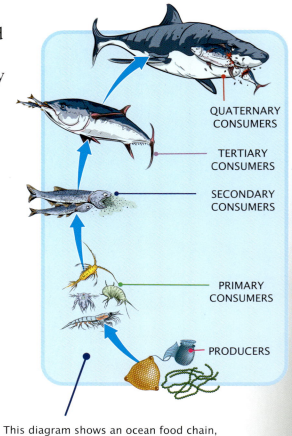

This diagram shows an ocean food chain, starting with tiny energy-producers. Not all ocean food chains have the same number of links: for example, some huge animals, such as the blue whale, eat tiny primary consumers.

About 1 cm (0.4 in) long, the black prince copepod is a species of zooplankton. It is an arthropod with an exoskeleton so thin we can see through it.

BIGGEST APEX PREDATORS

Sperm whale: Up to 20.5 m (67.3 ft) long

Orca, also known as the killer whale: Up to 9.8 m (32.2 ft) long

Saltwater crocodile: Up to 6.3 m (20.7 ft) long

Great white shark: Up to 6.1 m (20 ft) long

Tiger shark: Up to 5.5 m (18 ft) long

Tiger shark

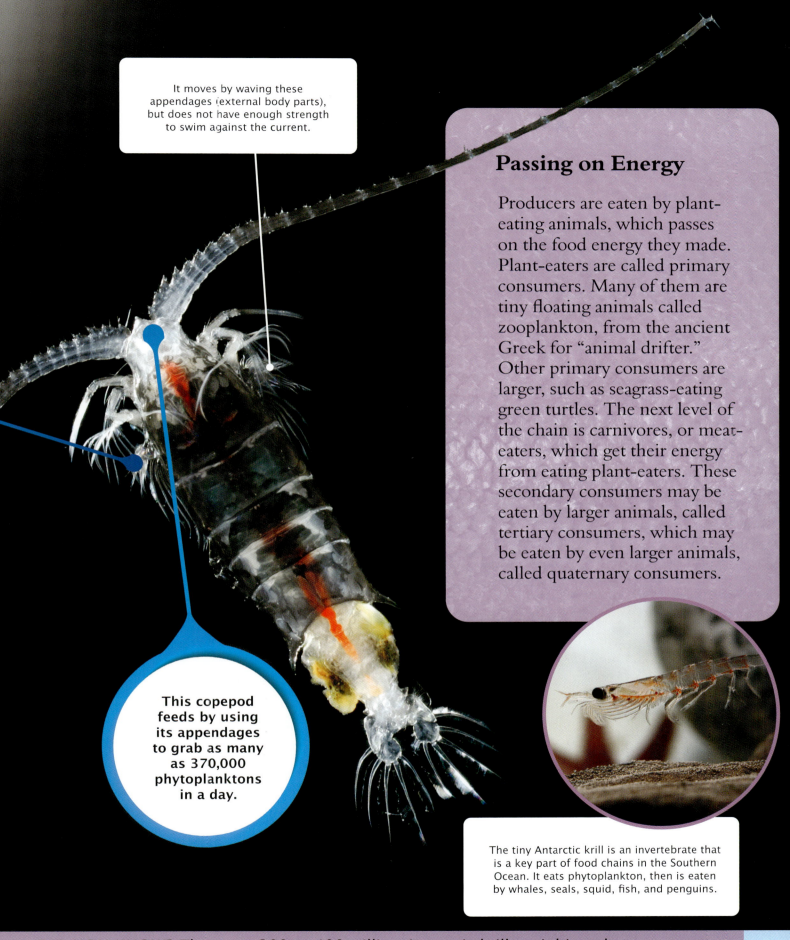

It moves by waving these appendages (external body parts), but does not have enough strength to swim against the current.

This copepod feeds by using its appendages to grab as many as 370,000 phytoplanktons in a day.

Passing on Energy

Producers are eaten by plant-eating animals, which passes on the food energy they made. Plant-eaters are called primary consumers. Many of them are tiny floating animals called zooplankton, from the ancient Greek for "animal drifter." Other primary consumers are larger, such as seagrass-eating green turtles. The next level of the chain is carnivores, or meat-eaters, which get their energy from eating plant-eaters. These secondary consumers may be eaten by larger animals, called tertiary consumers, which may be eaten by even larger animals, called quaternary consumers.

The tiny Antarctic krill is an invertebrate that is a key part of food chains in the Southern Ocean. It eats phytoplankton, then is eaten by whales, seals, squid, fish, and penguins.

DID YOU KNOW? There are 300 to 400 trillion Antarctic krill, weighing about 500 million tonnes (550 million tons)—making them the planet's weightiest species.

Predators and Prey

> The harlequin ghost pipefish is almost impossible to spot as it floats among the frondy arms of invertebrates called crinoids and gorgonians.

More than half of marine animals are predators, spending much of their time hunting for other animals to eat. Predators have evolved to have features and behaviors that make them good hunters. At the same time, their prey have developed their own special defenses.

Hunting Techniques

There are two main methods of catching prey: ambush and pursuit. Ambush predators sit and wait for prey, then pounce at the last moment. Ambush predators are often well camouflaged, so they blend into their environment. Some burrow into the ocean floor or hide in crevices. Pursuit predators, such as dolphins, chase after their prey, so they must be fast.

The sargassum fish is a well-camouflaged ambush predator that lives among sargassum seaweed. It uses a long growth on its head as a "lure" to attract fish and shrimp, then sucks them into its mouth.

MEGA-SHOALS
Estimated shoal size

Atlantic herring: Up to 4 billion fish

Pacific sardine: Up to 300 million fish

Peruvian anchovy: Up to 100 million fish

Atlantic mackerel: Up to 1 million fish

A sardine shoal

DID YOU KNOW? Spinner dolphins work together to capture fish, circling a shoal and then moving slowly inwards until the fish are tightly packed.

Defensive Techniques

One way to avoid being eaten is to go unnoticed, so many marine animals are camouflaged, while others are active only at night. Another defensive method is to live in a group. Some fish move in groups called shoals, giving them a greater chance of spotting predators and cutting down the chance of any single fish being eaten. Some animals make themselves difficult to catch or eat: octopus distract predators by releasing clouds of dark ink, while some sea urchins are covered in sharp spines. A few animals, such as pufferfish, are poisonous, so no predator will try the species twice.

The mimic octopus has a very unusual defense: it positions and moves its body to pretend to be more dangerous species, such as sea snakes. This one is pretending to be a poisonous flatfish.

This pipefish is almost transparent, but over a few hours it can change its color to match a new background.

Its camouflage is useful as a defense and while waiting to ambush shrimp, which it sucks into its tube-shaped mouth.

25

Ocean Life at Risk

The humphead wrasse is endangered by overfishing and damage to its coral reef habitat caused by global warming.

Human activities have damaged ocean habitats and reduced the numbers of many ocean species. As a result, around 2,270 marine animals are at risk of extinction. Many of these animals are called "endangered" species, while those very close to being wiped out are "critically endangered."

Damaged Habitats

When humans burn fuels such as coal and oil, we release "greenhouse gases" such as carbon dioxide into the atmosphere. These gases trap the Sun's heat and raise the Earth's temperature, like in a glass greenhouse. This global warming is slowly heating the oceans, making ice melt at the poles and damaging coral reefs. Other habitat damage is caused by rubbish, spills of chemicals, and building along coasts, which can destroy nesting sites.

The smalltooth sawfish lives along warm coasts of the Atlantic Ocean. It is critically endangered by habitat damage and fishing. This baby was born in an aquarium and is being released into the ocean to help grow the numbers of wild sawfish.

Hunting and Fishing

Some marine animals have been driven to extinction by human hunting, including the Atlantic Ocean gray whales, which died out in the eighteenth century. Today, the hunting of whales and other threatened species is banned by most countries. However, fish that are often eaten by humans can still suffer from overfishing. This is when so many fish are caught that the remaining adults cannot have babies fast enough to maintain the species.

The Atlantic cod was overfished in the 1990s, so today governments set limits on how many fish can be caught.

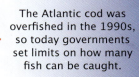

Although it is illegal to hunt the critically endangered Kemp's ridley sea turtle, it is often accidentally trapped and killed in nets for catching shrimp.

26

Using its lips, the wrasse carries sea urchins to a rock, where it cracks them open.

Some female wrasses turn into males at around nine years old, probably because older, bigger males can father more babies than older females can produce.

THREATENED SEABIRDS
Of around 1,500 threatened bird species

Balearic shearwater: Construction of hotels in its island habitat
Cape gannet: Lack of food due to human overfishing
Northern rockhopper penguin: Global warming, pollution, and overfishing
Spoonbilled sandpiper: Loss of its coastal habitats to industry
Waved albatross: Accidental capture in fishing lines

A pair of mating Cape gannets greet each other.

DID YOU KNOW? Water expands as it gets warmer, so scientists predict that sea levels will rise by anything from 26 to 270 cm (10 in to 8.8 ft) by the year 2100.

Chapter 2: Ocean Habitats

Ocean Zones

All living things are adapted to their surroundings, or habitat. In the ocean, the two key things that affect habitat are sunlight and temperature. Animals and plants that live in bright, warm waters could not survive in the darkest, coldest depths.

Temperature Zones

The ocean is warmest close to the equator, where it is heated most strongly by the Sun's rays. All over the world, surface waters are warmer than the waters beneath, as sunlight cannot penetrate farther than 1,000 m (3,300 ft) into the deep.

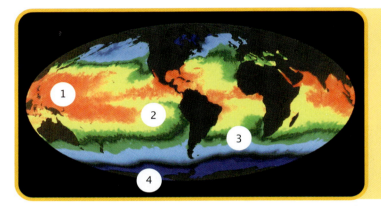

Ocean Climates
This map shows the average temperature at the water surface, from warm (red) to cold (blue).

KEY
1. **Tropical:** Water warm year round
2. **Subtropical:** Water fairly warm year round
3. **Temperate:** Water ranges from cold to warm
4. **Polar:** Water cold year round

Depth Zones

The sunlit surface waters are rich with life. Here, plants and chromists make their food from sunlight. These provide food for plant-eaters, which are eaten in their turn by bigger species. In the deep, dark ocean, there is no plant life and far fewer animals.

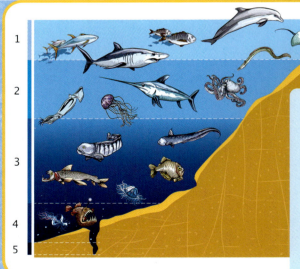

1. **SUNLIGHT ZONE:**
   0 to 200 m (0 to 660 ft)
   Most ocean plants and animals live here.

2. **TWILIGHT ZONE:**
   200 to 1,000 m (660 to 3,300 ft)
   Some animals travel from these dim waters to feed near the surface at night.

3. **MIDNIGHT ZONE:**
   1,000 to 4,000 m (3,300 to 13,000 ft)
   In total darkness, many animals are bioluminescent, or make their own light.

4. **ABYSSAL ZONE:**
   4,000 m (13,000 ft) to ocean floor
   Most animals have special features to survive the cold.

5. **HADAL ZONE:**
   Deep trenches
   Only a few species are known to survive here.

DEPTH AND TEMPERATURE RECORDS

Deepest trench: Mariana Trench, Pacific Ocean, 11,034 m (36,201 ft)
Shallowest ocean: Arctic Ocean, average depth 1,038 m (3,406 ft)
Coldest water: −2°C (28.4°F), Arctic and Southern Oceans
Hottest water: 35°C (95°F), in summer on the coasts of the Persian Gulf, Indian Ocean

Abu Dhabi, Persian Gulf

Many ocean animals are suited to a small range of temperatures and depths. Bigeye tuna are unusual because they can survive in deeper, colder waters and warm surface waters.

The bigeye tuna descends and rises as it follows its prey, such as sardines.

Its large eyes allow the tuna to see when it swims as deep as 500 m (1,650 ft).

DID YOU KNOW? Seawater turns to ice at −2°C (28.4°F) because the salt lowers its freezing point below that of freshwater (0°C/32°F).

29

Beaches

Sandy or muddy beaches are challenging habitats. Animals and plants must survive being plunged underwater by rising tides and breaking waves, then being exposed to the Sun and wind as the water draws back.

Tides

All beaches have daily high tides, when the sea washes up the shore, and low tides, when the sea draws back out. Tides are caused by gravity. Gravity pulls all objects toward each other, with larger objects, like planets and moons, having the greatest pull. As the Moon pulls on Earth, the sea bulges toward it. As the Earth turns, the moving bulge creates rising and falling tides.

This sand hopper burrows into the sand during high tide, but comes out when the tide is low to feed on washed-up seaweed.

Surviving the Intertidal Zone

Animals living in the intertidal zone, the area between the high and low tide lines, have to survive dramatic changes in their habitat. Some beach animals, such as birds, move up the beach when the tide rises. Others burrow into the sand, choosing wet sand if they need to stay damp. Some insects, such as dune chafer and sandgraver beetles, shelter in the seaweed and driftwood found at the high tide line.

The lugworm burrows in damp sand. It eats sand, digesting the microorganisms it contains, then poops out a coiled "cast" of used sand.

SANDERLING
Calidris alba

Length: 18 to 21 cm (7 to 8 in)
Range: Arctic in summer; Americas, Africa, Europe, Asia, and Australasia in winter
Habitat: Sandy and rocky beaches
Diet: Buried invertebrates, including arthropods, molluscs, and worms
Conservation: Not at risk

A sanderling pulls a bloodworm from the sand.

This crab lives on tropical beaches of the Indian and Pacific Oceans.

The horn-eyed ghost crab's eyes are on stalks, which can be folded down when it is burrowing.

The crab uses its claws to burrow into the sand, so it can hide during the day.

DID YOU KNOW? Tiny mole crabs can completely bury themselves under sand in just 1.5 seconds.

Rocky Shores

Sea cliffs offer resting and nesting spaces for many species of seabirds. On rocky beaches, battered by the waves, lots of animals have hard shells for protection. Many of them attach to the rocks so they are not dragged out to sea.

Clinging On

Hard-shelled invertebrates are often found clinging to rocks and other surfaces in the intertidal zone. These include bivalves, such as mussels and oysters, which have two-part shells that open and close for protection. They use a muscly foot to dig into the seafloor or they attach themselves to rocks with a sticky thread called byssus. Other groups of clingers-on include the single-shelled limpets and the barnacles, with shells usually made of six plates.

Pale-shelled goose barnacles and blue mussels wait for the tide to rise, so they can feed on tiny creatures in the water.

Limpets are snails that move by rippling the muscles of their foot. When the tide is low, they attach themselves tightly to rocks so they do not dry out.

Rock Pools

At low tide, pools of water are left behind in dips and crevices in the rocks. The animals, plants, and chromists that live in them must be able to survive sudden changes in temperature, blasts of wind, and drying out in the sun. If the pool empties, green algae may provide the only shelter, as seabirds swoop to find food.

Invertebrates in this rock pool include ochre starfish, purple sea urchins, and sea anemones.

SEA SLATER
Ligia oceanica

Length: 2.5 to 3 cm (1 to 1.2 in)
Range: Temperate coasts of Europe and North America
Habitat: Rock pools and crevices on rocky beaches
Diet: Seaweed and diatoms
Conservation: Not at risk

Sea slater

Common murres spend most of their lives at sea, returning to land only to nest on rocky cliffs.

Murres nest in large colonies, or groups, which are known as loomeries.

These seabirds use their wings to "swim" underwater as they chase cod and herring.

DID YOU KNOW? There are at least 12,000 species of seaweeds, which are plant-like organisms known as algae.

33

Mangrove Forests

Mangroves are trees that can live in saltwater. They are often found along tropical and subtropical coasts where the water is shallow and calm. Fish and invertebrates shelter among the mangroves' roots, while birds perch on branches as they watch for prey.

Archerfish

In a mangrove forest, ocean meets land in a unique habitat. Archerfish are among the species that have evolved to make full use of this mix. These fish catch insects that are sitting on branches overhanging the water by firing jets of water at them. Archerfish do this by sucking in water, pressing their tongue against the roof of their mouth to form a tube, then spitting.

A banded archerfish shoots a jet of water at a cricket. When the cricket falls into the water, it will be snapped up.

Red mangroves are among the most common species of mangrove trees.

Mudskippers

These fish have developed extraordinary features that allow them to survive in the intertidal zone of mangrove forests. At low tide, mudskippers use their strong pectoral fins to drag themselves across the exposed mud. While most fish cannot breathe out of water, mudskippers can soak up oxygen from the air through their skin, as long as they stay wet by rolling in puddles.

A mudskipper's eyes move separately from each other, so the fish can see above and below water at the same time.

DID YOU KNOW? The banded archerfish can aim jets of water at prey sitting up to 3 m (9.8 ft) away.

Long, stilt-like roots allow the mangroves' branches and leaves to stay above the level of high tide.

Mangroves are often "nurseries" for young fish, which find hiding places and plenty of food among the roots and mud.

MANGROVE PITTA

Pitta megarhyncha

Length: 18 to 21 cm (7 to 8.3 in)

Range: Coasts of southern Asia

Habitat: Mangrove forests

Diet: Small crabs, snails, and insects

Conservation: Population shrinking due to habitat loss

Mangrove pitta

35

Kelp Forests

Kelps are plant-like algae that grow in cool, coastal waters. Where kelps grow thickly, they form a habitat called a kelp forest. These provide shelter from storms; hiding places from predators; and food for plant-eaters, which are in turn food for meat-eaters.

Giant kelp grows to more than 50 m (160 ft) long.

A Vital Habitat

Like an above-water forest of trees, kelp forests have a "canopy" formed by the tallest species, which grow up to the water surface. In the shade beneath, shorter species form a thick "understorey" and carpet the seafloor. Invertebrates, such as sea urchins, feed on the kelp itself. They are preyed on by kelp bass and other fish. These smaller creatures are food for mammals including seals, sea lions, otters, and gray whales. Birds such as gulls and cormorants swoop at the surface.

The kelp bass lives in kelp forests, where it feeds on small fish, squid, and shrimp.

A bat ray swims through a kelp forest off the coast of California, USA.

WESTERN SPINY BRITTLE STAR

Ophiothrix spiculata

Length: 18 to 38 cm (7 to 15 in)
Range: Pacific Ocean from southern USA to Peru
Habitat: Sandy seafloor, often around kelp, to depths of 2,000 m (6,500 ft)
Diet: Small invertebrates and microorganisms
Conservation: Not at risk

Western spiny brittle stars

DID YOU KNOW? Growing at up to 60 cm (2 ft) per day, giant kelp is one of the fastest-growing living things in the world.

Kelp anchors itself in the seabed with a root-like structure called a "holdfast."

Decorator Crabs

Many animals hide away in kelp forests, but the graceful decorator crab uses a more unusual form of camouflage. It attaches kelp and other living things, such as sponges, to hooks on its shell, so it can disguise itself.

With strips of kelp on its back, this graceful decorator crab is hoping to hide from predators such as sea otters.

Seagrass Meadows

There are around 60 species of seagrasses, which can cover the seafloor rather like meadows of grass on land. These plants need sunlight to photosynthesize, so they grow in clear, shallow waters. They are found from the equator nearly all the way to the North and South Poles.

Fish Nurseries

Many fish use seagrass meadows as nurseries, where eggs are released and young fish can grow safely, hiding from predators among the grass. When the fish grow into adults, many swim away to a range of habitats, from nearby coral reefs to the vast ocean. Other fish, often small and well-camouflaged species such as seahorses, stay among the seagrass for life.

Precious Habitat

Hundreds of species, from green turtles and manatees to sea urchins, feed on seagrass leaves and stems. Other animals use the grass as a hiding place as they lie in wait for prey. Among these ambush predators are fish such as the fierce and well-camouflaged moray eels and grass gobies. However, pollution and coastal construction are destroying seagrass meadows at a rate of two football fields every hour. Today, one-quarter of seagrass animals are at risk.

Found in the tropical Indian and Pacific Oceans, a young blue triggerfish is sheltered by seagrass.

Adult green sea turtles spend most of their time grazing in seagrass meadows.

A snowflake moray eel watches for shrimp and small crabs. It will snap them up with its powerful jaws, crushing their shells with its blunt teeth, then use an extra set of teeth, in its throat, for mashing them.

FLORAL BLENNY
Petroscirtes mitratus

Length: 8 to 8.5 cm (3.1 to 3.3 in)
Range: Tropical coasts of the Indian and Pacific Oceans
Habitat: Seagrass meadows and coral reefs
Diet: Algae, diatoms, and small crustaceans
Conservation: Population at risk in some regions

Floral blenny

The green sea turtle can grow to 1.5 m (5 ft) long.

The destruction of seagrass meadows, along with hunting and pollution, have put this turtle at risk of extinction.

DID YOU KNOW? The green sea turtle gets its name from the layer of green fat under its shell, caused by eating so much seagrass.

Coral Reefs

Coral reefs are home to one-quarter of all marine species. Reefs are rocky ridges built by stony corals. These invertebrates live in large groups called colonies. Reefs are found in shallow, tropical waters. Some coral species live in cold, deep water, but they do not build great reefs.

Building Reefs

Reefs are made of the skeletons of millions or billions of stony coral polyps. A polyp has a soft, cuplike body, armed with tentacles for catching food. Each polyp builds a hard skeleton around itself. When a polyp dies, its skeleton is left behind and a new polyp settles on top, growing the reef. Today, around two-thirds of coral reefs are at risk, as they are very sensitive to water temperature and pollution.

Up to 18 cm (7 in) long, the mirror butterflyfish feeds on coral polyps and small invertebrates.

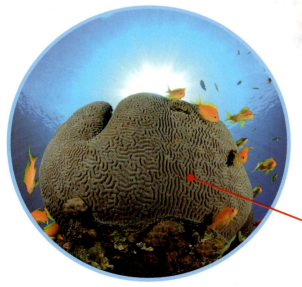

Brain corals are among more than 3,000 species of stony corals. Each brain coral is a colony of thousands of tiny, identical living polyps.

40   **DID YOU KNOW?** The world's largest coral reef system is the Great Barrier Reef, which stretches for over 2,300 km (1,400 miles) off the coast of Australia.

This is a soft coral colony, made up of tiny polyps that do not build a hard skeleton. Polyps are food for reef fish and invertebrates.

Bright Shades

Many reef fish and invertebrates are brightly patterned. For some, such as spotted trunkfish, the pattern warns other animals they are poisonous. Predators come to link that pattern with danger. Bright patterns are also useful for picking out other members of the same species for mating. For most reef species, their shades and patterns act as camouflage against the vivid, sun-dappled reef.

This day octopus is totally still as it waits for fish, crabs, or shrimp. In just a few seconds, it changes the shades and patterns on its skin to match the surrounding coral.

The emperor angelfish has bright blue and yellow stripes. It eats hard-to-chew sponges and algae with its large, strong jaws.

COPPERBAND BUTTERFLYFISH

Chelmon rostratus

Length: 18 to 20 cm (7 to 8 in)

Range: Tropical coasts of the Indian and Pacific Oceans

Habitat: Coral reefs and rocky shores

Diet: Sea anenomes, worms, and molluscs

Conservation: Not at risk

Copperband butterflyfish

41

Polar Waters

In winter, the surface of the Arctic Ocean and the sea surrounding Antarctica freezes. In summer, this sea ice melts and shrinks. Platforms of ice as thick as 1,000 m (3,300 ft), called ice shelves, extend into the ocean from the land. Sometimes, icebergs break off and float away.

Staying Warm

Animals that live in the Arctic and Southern Oceans must have special features to survive the cold. Mammals, such as seals and whales, have a thick layer of fat called blubber, which keeps in their body heat. They also have rounded bodies, with a smaller surface from which to lose heat. This has the same warming effect as huddling into a ball. Polar seabirds have a waterproof coat of tightly packed feathers.

Up to 2.3 m (7.5 ft) long, crabeater seals rest and mate on the sea ice around Antarctica.

Anti-Freeze Blood

Fish that live in the coldest waters need special defenses to stop their blood from freezing. Antarctic icefish blood contains a special substance called glycoprotein. It disturbs the molecules in the blood, stopping them from joining together and freezing into ice.

The blood of an icefish is thin and colorless, which makes the fish transparent.

Narwhals are toothed whales that live in the Arctic Ocean, feeding on fish beneath the sea ice.

ARCTIC TERN
Sterna paradisaea

Length: 28 to 39 cm (11 to 15 in)
Range: Arctic and northern temperate coasts in northern summer; Southern Ocean and coasts in southern summer
Habitat: Coasts, grassland, and oceans
Diet: Small fish, crabs, and krill
Conservation: Population shrinking due to habitat loss and overfishing

Arctic tern

Narwhals live in groups of up to 20, joining together into groups of up to 1,000 in summer.

Male narwhals have a spiral tusk up to 3.1 m (10.2 ft) long. It is a tooth that grows from the left side of the mouth, through the lip.

DID YOU KNOW? The bowhead whale, which lives in the Arctic Ocean, has the thickest blubber of any animal, up to 50 cm (20 in) thick.

Deep Ocean

In the midnight zone, the temperature is only around 4°C (39°F). With no light, there are no plants and no plant-eating animals. Many animals here are predators that hunt by smell and touch rather than by sight and speed. Some eat the dead plants and animals that sink to the seafloor.

Strange Bodies

Fish that spend some of their time in the twilight zone have huge eyes that can gather as much light as possible. Fish that never leave the midnight zone may be completely eyeless but have fins that are very sensitive to touch. Below 1,000 m (3,300 ft), many fish have small bodies, which need little food, and large mouths and stomachs to swallow whatever prey comes their way.

A gulper eel's huge mouth can open wide enough to swallow prey much larger than the eel itself.

HALF-NAKED HATCHETFISH

Argyropelecus hemigymnus

Length: 3 to 5 cm (1.2 to 2 in)
Range: Tropical to temperate Atlantic, Indian, and Pacific Oceans
Habitat: From depths of 200 to 2,400 m (650 to 7,870 ft)
Diet: Zooplankton
Conservation: Not at risk

Half-naked hatchetfish

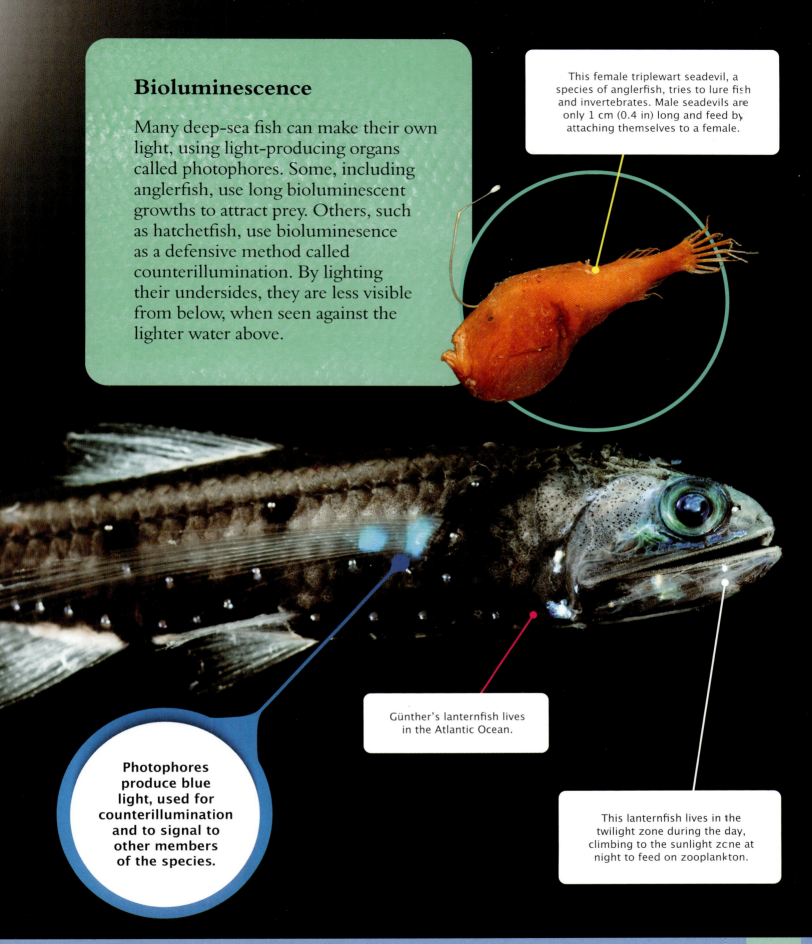

Bioluminescence

Many deep-sea fish can make their own light, using light-producing organs called photophores. Some, including anglerfish, use long bioluminescent growths to attract prey. Others, such as hatchetfish, use bioluminesence as a defensive method called counterillumination. By lighting their undersides, they are less visible from below, when seen against the lighter water above.

This female triplewart seadevil, a species of anglerfish, tries to lure fish and invertebrates. Male seadevils are only 1 cm (0.4 in) long and feed by attaching themselves to a female.

Günther's lanternfish lives in the Atlantic Ocean.

Photophores produce blue light, used for counterillumination and to signal to other members of the species.

This lanternfish lives in the twilight zone during the day, climbing to the sunlight zone at night to feed on zooplankton.

DID YOU KNOW? The scaly dragonfish, which lives as deep as 1,500 m (4,900 ft), can turn its bioluminescence on and off to confuse predators.

Hydrothermal Vents

The Earth's surface is made from giant plates of rock that move slowly against each other, sometimes causing earthquakes and volcanoes. Hydrothermal vents are cracks in the seafloor, above the plate edges. Water heated in the Earth's super-hot interior rises through the vents.

Hotspots for Life

A hydrothermal vent offers a completely different habitat from the surrounding seafloor. The water from a vent ranges from 60°C to 460°C (140°F to 860°F). The water is also rich in minerals, such as sulphur, from inside the Earth. Special bacteria use the sulphur to make their own food. Other animals, most of them found only around vents, eat the bacteria and each other.

This vent is 3,300 m (10,800 ft) below the surface of the Atlantic Ocean. It is called a "black smoker" because minerals in the water have slowly built rocky chimneys, which belch out black, sulphur-rich water.

Giant tube worms attach themselves to the seabed. Their red "plume," which collects sulphur from the water, is pulled inside the protective tube if a predator arrives.

Giant Tube Worms

Giant tube worms live only around sulphur-rich vents on the Pacific Ocean floor. They get their food by taking bacteria into their skin, rather like getting an infection. The bacteria make their home inside the worms, where they turn sulphur into food, which the worms share.

HYDROTHERMAL THREE-BEARDED ROCKLING

Gaidropsarus mauli

Length: 25 to 30 cm (10 to 12 in)
Range: Lucky Strike Vents, Mid-Atlantic Ridge, Atlantic Ocean
Habitat: From depths of 900 to 1,700 m (300 to 5,500 ft) around vents
Diet: Shrimp and other invertebrates
Conservation: Not at risk

This species of rockling was discovered in 2018.

Galatheid crabs feed on bacteria.

Using remote-controlled submarines, researchers have discovered many new species of shrimp living around hydrothermal vents.

These hydrothermal mussels have attached to the seafloor beside the Champagne Vent, on the floor of the Pacific Ocean.

DID YOU KNOW? Giant tube worms, which live in colonies of many hundred worms, can grow to 2.4 m (7.9 ft) long.

Chapter 3: Shark Life
Super Sharks

Sharks are an extraordinary group of fish. Some sharks are famed for their ferocity, while others are known for their great size or speed. Nearly all sharks are meat-eaters, swallowing animals from seals to seabirds and shrimp to other sharks.

The little gulper shark hunts for fish and squid in coastal waters.

Hunters

Most sharks are hunters, using their keen senses to track down prey. The majority of fish have small brains compared to their body size, but sharks have fairly large brains. Having a larger brain helps sharks to make sense of information from their senses. It also helps them plan where and how to catch prey. A few sharks can even work with other members of their group to corner and catch prey.

This small shark grows up to 1 m (3.3 ft) long.

Of all the sharks, the shortfin mako shark has one of the largest brains compared to its body size. It stalks its prey unnoticed, waiting for a moment when fish are weakest.

Habitats

Most sharks live in the oceans, but a few can survive in both salty ocean water and freshwater rivers. Sharks are found in all oceans, from warm tropical waters through cooler temperate seas to the cold polar zone. Sharks are common fish down to 2,000 m (6,560 ft) beneath the ocean surface. A few sharks are known to swim as deep as 3,000 m (9,840 ft). While some sharks are found in the open ocean, far from land, others live only in coastal habitats, including coral reefs and seagrass meadows.

Around 64 cm (25 in) long, the blind shark lives in seagrass meadows on the eastern coast of Australia.

Its green eyes are large, helping it to see in the dim water up to 1,400 m (4,600 ft) beneath the ocean surface.

Divers take a close look at a great white shark while protected by a cage.

Humans

Since humans first journeyed over the oceans, we have been fascinated by sharks. From the islands of the Pacific Ocean to the coasts of Africa, people's fear and wonder of sharks led them to worship shark gods. In more recent times, movies have told tales of terrifying sharks with a taste for human flesh. Yet the truth is that sharks have far more to fear from humans than we do from them. Today, sharks are at risk due to human activities from fishing to construction.

49

What Is a Shark?

Like all fish, sharks can breathe underwater, have scale-covered skin, and use their fins for swimming. Yet while most fish have skeletons made of bone, sharks and their relatives have skeletons made of cartilage.

A Shark Skeleton

Cartilage is a body material that is less hard than bone, but much more bendy and lightweight. Humans have cartilage in places such as their outer ears and the tip of their nose. Cartilage makes a shark's skeleton lighter than those of similarly sized fish, so it can use less energy to swim. In addition, cartilage helps a shark to twist and turn easily.

A shark has no ribcage to protect its organs, but its fins are supported by cartilage.

Great white shark

LARGEST SHARKS

Whale shark: Up to 18.8 m (61.7 ft) long
Basking shark: Up to 12.3 m (40.3 ft) long
Greenland shark: Up to 6.4 m (21 ft) long
Great white shark: Up to 6.1 m (20 ft) long
Great hammerhead shark: Up to 6.1 m (20 ft) long

DID YOU KNOW? Sharks have no ribcage, so if they wash up on shore their organs can be crushed by the weight of their body.

A whale shark can weigh around 19,000 kg (42,000 lb), which is more than 270 adult men.

Biggest and Smallest

The largest shark is also the world's largest fish. The whale shark can grow up to 18.8 m (61.7 ft) long. It is found throughout the world's tropical oceans. In contrast, the smallest shark is found only along the coasts of Venezuela and Colombia, in South America. The dwarf lanternshark grows no longer than 20 cm (8 in). It is believed to live for 20 to 30 years, while its immense relative may live for up to 130 years.

Like most other fish, a Pacific double-saddle butterflyfish has a bony skeleton.

Like all sharks, a blacktip reef shark has flexible jaws that are not attached to its skull, so it can shoot them forward to snap up prey.

A close relative of sharks, a stingray also has a skeleton made of cartilage.

51

Anatomy

Most sharks have eight fins, but some have fewer. Like other fish, sharks breathe using gills. While the gills of most fish are protected by a bony cover, sharks have visible gill slits on either side of their head. Most sharks have five pairs of gill slits, but some have six or seven.

Fins

All sharks have a pair of pectoral fins, on either side of their body behind their head. These large fins help with steering. On a shark's underside, it has a pair of pelvic fins, which aid stability by stopping sideways rolls. Most sharks also have a single anal fin closer to their tail, which improves stability. Sharks have either one or two dorsal fins on their upper side, with the first dorsal fin larger than the second. Dorsal fins keep the shark upright. The tail fin, known as the caudal fin, is moved from side to side to push the shark forward. The upper portion, or lobe, of the caudal fin is usually larger than the lower lobe.

The Atlantic sixgill is a rare shark, found only in the warm waters of the western Atlantic Ocean.

A Caribbean reef shark has eight fins and five pairs of gill slits.

- First dorsal fin
- Second dorsal fin
- Gill slits
- Caudal fin
- Anal fin
- Pelvic fins
- Pectoral fins

Tiger shark tooth

BIGGEST TEETH

Great white shark: 6.4 cm (2.5 in) long, around 250 at a time
Tiger shark: 5.1 cm (2 in) long, around 350 at a time
Sand tiger shark: 2.5 cm (1 in) long, around 150 at a time
Bull shark: 2.5 cm (1 in) long, around 350 at a time
Shortfin mako shark: 2 cm (0.8 in), around 100 at a time

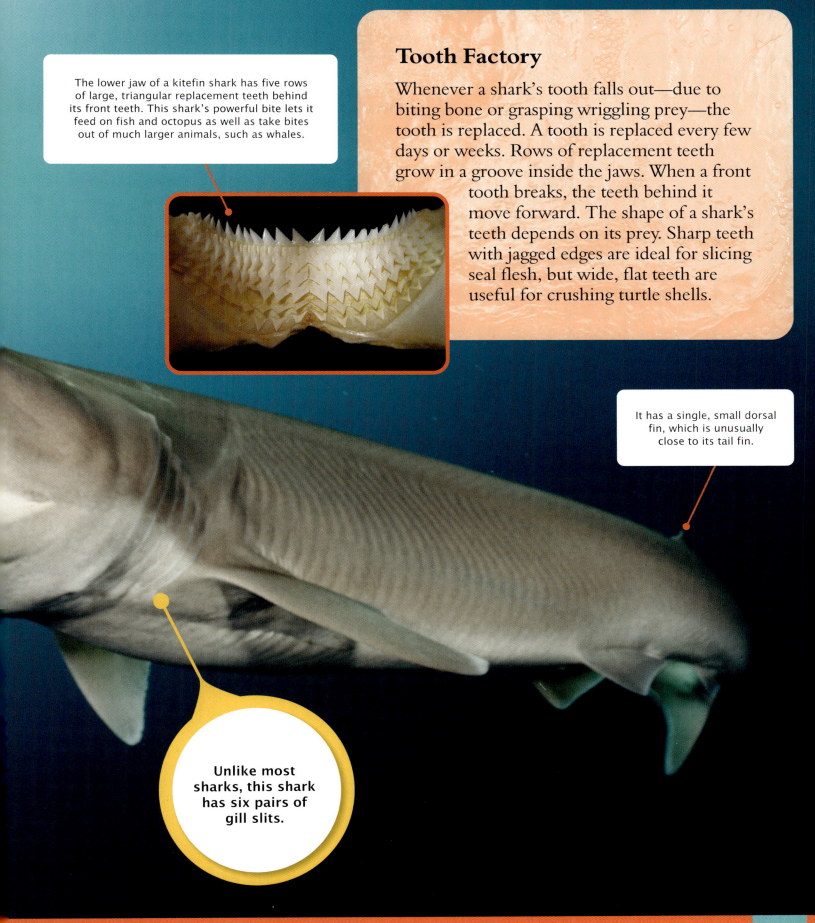

The lower jaw of a kitefin shark has five rows of large, triangular replacement teeth behind its front teeth. This shark's powerful bite lets it feed on fish and octopus as well as take bites out of much larger animals, such as whales.

Tooth Factory

Whenever a shark's tooth falls out—due to biting bone or grasping wriggling prey—the tooth is replaced. A tooth is replaced every few days or weeks. Rows of replacement teeth grow in a groove inside the jaws. When a front tooth breaks, the teeth behind it move forward. The shape of a shark's teeth depends on its prey. Sharp teeth with jagged edges are ideal for slicing seal flesh, but wide, flat teeth are useful for crushing turtle shells.

It has a single, small dorsal fin, which is unusually close to its tail fin.

Unlike most sharks, this shark has six pairs of gill slits.

DID YOU KNOW? Ground sharks can grow as many as 35,000 teeth over the course of their life.

53

Skin

Shark skin is thicker than the skin of other fish, which helps protect sharks from attacks by predators. Their skin is also so rough that it can injure an attacker. Shark skin is almost entirely covered with special, toothlike scales known as dermal denticles.

Dermal Denticles

Sharks and their relatives have dermal denticles, which means "small skin teeth." These scales contain similar materials to human teeth, such as enamel, which makes them very hard. The scales are ribbed and pointed. When stroked backward, the scales are sharp, but they are flattened by the flow of water as a shark swims. The shape of the scales helps a shark to cut through the water swiftly and silently, so it can creep up on prey.

The banded wobbegong is nocturnal, doing most of its feeding at night.

Under a powerful microscope, we can see the dermal denticles of the small-spotted catshark. Each denticle is up to 1 mm (0.04 in) long.

The tasselled wobbegong is a carpet shark that is well camouflaged on coral reefs.

Camouflage

Many sharks have patterned dermal denticles to help with camouflage. This lets them blend in with their surroundings, making them difficult for predators and prey to spot. In the carpet shark order, many sharks have bold patterns to blend in when lying among coral or on the seabed. Sharks that live in open water, such as the great white shark, may be countershaded, with pale undersides and darker backs. From below, the pale belly is hard to spot against the sunlight. From above, the shark blends into the darker depths.

54

DEEPEST DIVES

Portuguese dogfish: 3,675 m (12,057 ft) deep
Cookiecutter shark: 3,505 m (11,500 ft) deep
Velvet belly lanternshark: 2,490 m (8,170 ft) deep
Greenland shark: 2,200 m (7,200 ft) deep
Pacific sleeper shark: 2,000 m (6,600 ft) deep

Greenland shark

This shark lies in wait as flaps of skin around its mouth drift in the water, attracting the attention of small prey.

Inside the mouth are more than 100 long, sharp teeth.

DID YOU KNOW? The skin of a whale shark is up to 15 cm (4 in) thick, the thickest of any animal.

Breathing

Like all animals, a shark needs a constant supply of oxygen for its organs to function. Water contains oxygen, which sharks take in using their gills. To breathe, sharks can open their mouth while swimming, so water flows inside, passes through the gills, and runs out of the gill slits.

Taking Oxygen

Like other fish, a shark uses its gills for taking in oxygen and getting rid of carbon dioxide, which is a waste product made by the body as it turns oxygen into energy. After water flows into a shark's mouth, it passes into the gills through openings at the sides of the mouth. The water flows over feather-like filaments that contain many tiny blood vessels. These have such thin walls that oxygen can pass through and into the shark's blood.

> The coral catshark spends the daytime resting in crevices on coral reefs, in the Indian and Pacific Oceans.

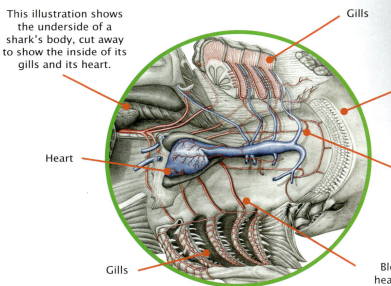

This illustration shows the underside of a shark's body, cut away to show the inside of its gills and its heart.

Heart

Gills

Gills

Sharks breathe by taking in water through their mouth. Although sharks do have nostrils, they are used only for smelling.

Blood containing carbon dioxide flows to the heart and is pumped to the gills, where the gas is released.

Blood containing oxygen flows to the heart, which pumps it around the body.

LONGEST LIVING SHARKS

Greenland shark: Over 270 years
Whale shark: Over 100 years
Bluntnose sixgill shark: Over 80 years
Great white shark: Over 70 years
Spiny dogfish: Over 45 years

Spiny dogfish

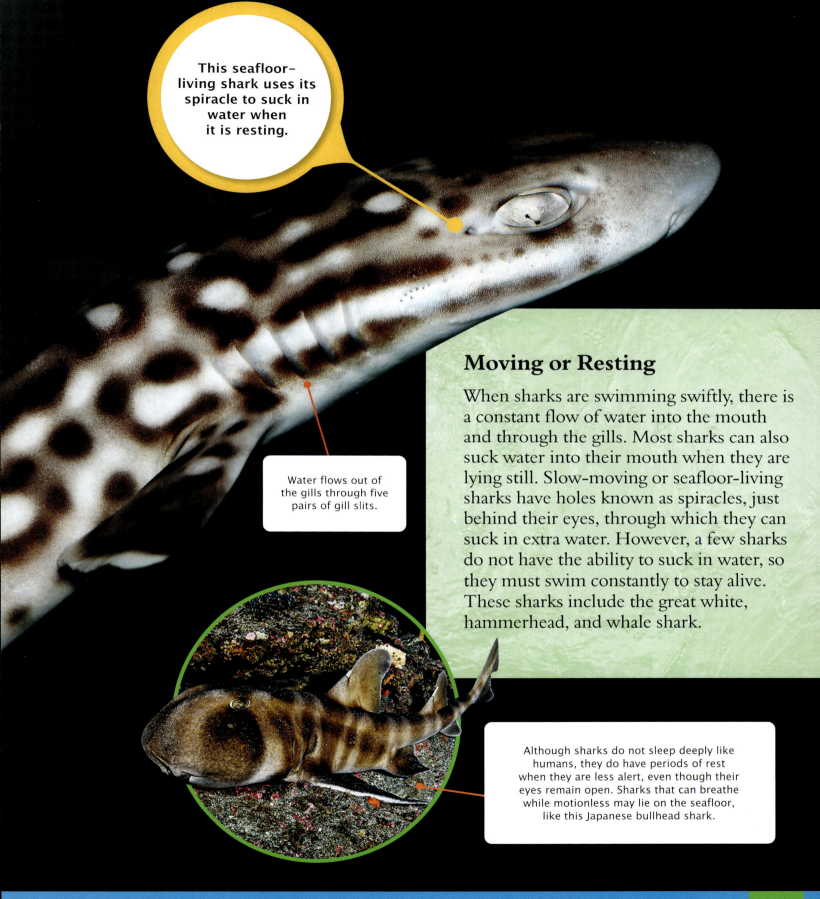

This seafloor-living shark uses its spiracle to suck in water when it is resting.

Water flows out of the gills through five pairs of gill slits.

Moving or Resting

When sharks are swimming swiftly, there is a constant flow of water into the mouth and through the gills. Most sharks can also suck water into their mouth when they are lying still. Slow-moving or seafloor-living sharks have holes known as spiracles, just behind their eyes, through which they can suck in extra water. However, a few sharks do not have the ability to suck in water, so they must swim constantly to stay alive. These sharks include the great white, hammerhead, and whale shark.

Although sharks do not sleep deeply like humans, they do have periods of rest when they are less alert, even though their eyes remain open. Sharks that can breathe while motionless may lie on the seafloor, like this Japanese bullhead shark.

DID YOU KNOW? Even when a great white shark is sleeping, it will continue to swim as its fin movements are automatic.

Swimming

Unlike most fish, a shark will sink if it stops swimming. This is useful for bottom-living sharks, but not so useful for sharks that hunt in open water. Yet sharks are expert swimmers, moving their fins to travel up, down, left, right, and forward—but never backward.

Staying Afloat

Fish with bony skeletons are able to float because of a gas-filled organ named a swim bladder, which acts like an air-filled rubber ring. Sharks do not have swim bladders. However, they do have a lightweight skeleton. In addition, they have a large liver, which is filled with oil. This oil is lighter than seawater, enabling a shark to float a little. Yet sharks would still sink slowly in the water, so they must swim constantly to stay at a particular depth, using the position of their pectoral fins to steer themselves upward.

A shark's pectoral fins function a little like the wings of a plane. The fins' shape and tilt make the water flow more quickly over them than beneath them. This puts greater water pressure on the underside of a shark's pectoral fins, pushing the shark upward.

FASTEST SWIMMERS

Shortfin mako shark: Up to 74 km/h (46 miles per hour)
Salmon shark: Up to 56 km/h (35 miles per hour)
Common thresher shark: Up to 48 km/h (30 miles per hour)
Great white shark: Up to 40 km/h (25 miles per hour)
Blue shark: Up to 39 km/h (24.5 miles per hour)

Thresher shark

DID YOU KNOW? The slowest shark, the Greenland shark beats its tail only 9 times per minute and reaches 3 km/h (1.9 miles per hour).

The tall dorsal fin acts as a pivot (like the middle point of a seesaw), letting the shark spin quickly around it.

A tiger shark swims by beating its tail from side to side.

Its long pectoral fins lift this shark—which weighs up to 635 kg (1,400 lb)—through the water.

No Going Back

Sharks have different styles of swimming, but no shark can swim backward. Solid-bodied sharks, such as great whites, swim by beating their large tail. Sharks with long, slender bodies, such as catsharks, also wiggle their body from side to side, like an eel. All these movements push a shark forward rather than backward. A shark's pectoral fins do not have the range of movement needed to paddle a shark backward. Sharks can move backward only by turning around or letting themselves drift.

A striped pyjama catshark wiggles its whole body in a wave-like motion.

Senses

Sharks have the same five senses as humans: sight, hearing, taste, smell, and touch. In addition, sharks can sense electrical currents and changes in water pressure. All these senses make sharks skilled hunters—as well as helping smaller sharks to escape attack.

Seven Senses

> The blue shark's sense of smell is less powerful than its eyesight, with only 3 percent of its brain dedicated to examining smells.

① **Sight:** A shark has eyes on the sides of its head, so it can see all around. At the back of each eye is a layer of shiny cells, which reflects light back into the eye, helping a shark to see in dark, deep water.

② **Hearing:** A shark's ears are behind its eyes, visible from the outside as two small holes. Sharks are particularly good at hearing low sounds, such as the noises made by wounded prey.

③ **Taste:** Most sharks do not rely on taste to find prey, so this sense is usually less developed than the others. However, some sharks have barbels (see opposite). All sharks taste prey when they bite in, spitting out what they do not like.

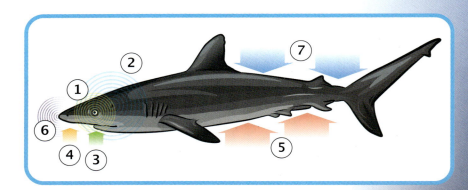

④ **Smell:** This sense is one of a shark's most powerful, with large parts of its brain devoted to identifying smells. Tiny particles given off by prey and predators float through the water to a shark's nostrils. A shark can sense the direction of a smell from the time that it reaches each nostril.

⑤ **Touch:** Nerves in a shark's skin and teeth carry signals about touch, temperature, and pain to its brain. The sensitivity of its teeth means that a shark often uses its mouth to find out more about objects.

⑥ **Electroreception:** A shark's snout and head have many tiny dips, or pores, known as ampullae of Lorenzini. These contain special cells that detect electric fields. As any animal's muscles move, they give off tiny electric charges. Sharks are more sensitive to these electric fields than any other animal.

⑦ **Pressure changes:** A line of pores, known as the lateral line, runs from a shark's snout to its tail. As water flows into these pores, special cells sense changes in the pressure of the water. This lets a shark detect moving prey and understand its surroundings, as its movement creates waves that bounce back off rocks and the seabed.

DID YOU KNOW? Around 18 percent of a great white shark's brain is dedicated to smell, giving it one of the most powerful senses of smell of all sharks.

With its two barbels, the zebra shark can hunt for small fish and shrimp at night.

Barbels

Some sharks have fleshy, finger-like body parts on their snout, known as barbels. These are sense organs a little like a cat's whiskers. Barbels are usually found on fish that live in murky water or hunt at night, helping them make up for loss of vision. Barbels have cells that detect particles that float from prey and predators, improving the closely linked senses of taste and smell.

Its eyes are large, so they can let in enough light for the shark to see in dim water as deep as 350 m (1,150 ft).

Ampullae of Lorenzini are dotted across the snout, helping the blue shark detect the movements of squid and octopus.

The bigeye thresher has the largest eyes of any shark, up to 10 cm (4 in) across.

SENSING PREY
Maximum distances for sharks

Smell: Up to 500 m (1,640 ft)
Hearing: Up to 240 m (790 ft)
Pressure changes: Up to 100 m (330 ft)
Sight: Up to 25 m (80 ft)
Electroreception: Up to 0.9 m (3 ft)

Feeding

Most sharks feed every two or three days. Although sharks are excellent at finding prey, their bodies are slow at digesting (breaking down) food, so they must wait between meals. All except three sharks are hunters that use their strong teeth for catching and killing.

Hunting Methods

Some sharks, such as great whites, use speed and strength to catch large prey. In contrast, seafloor-living sharks such as wobbegongs and angelsharks use camouflage and patience, lying in wait for prey, then making a sudden lunge. Sawsharks use their long snout to stir up small prey from the seabed, while thresher sharks stun fish with flicks of their large tail. Cookiecutter sharks rarely take whole prey, but feed on flesh bitten from living animals.

Copper sharks hunt in a group, working together to herd fish into a ball. Each shark takes turns to swim through the ball with its mouth open.

When a great white shark bites a fish, the strength of its jaws and sharpness of its teeth can kill instantly.

A copper shark grows up to 3.3 m (11 ft) long.

DID YOU KNOW? Copper sharks swim around fishermen in the hope of stealing their catches, even attempting to snatch fish from their hands.

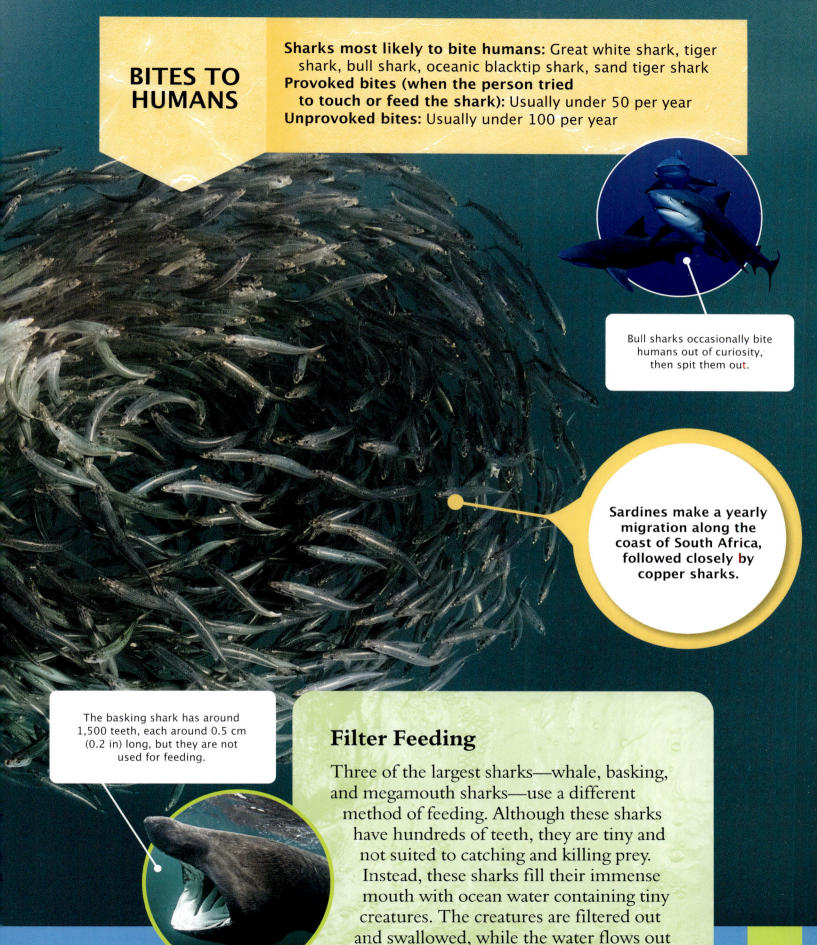

BITES TO HUMANS

Sharks most likely to bite humans: Great white shark, tiger shark, bull shark, oceanic blacktip shark, sand tiger shark
Provoked bites (when the person tried to touch or feed the shark): Usually under 50 per year
Unprovoked bites: Usually under 100 per year

Bull sharks occasionally bite humans out of curiosity, then spit them out.

Sardines make a yearly migration along the coast of South Africa, followed closely by copper sharks.

The basking shark has around 1,500 teeth, each around 0.5 cm (0.2 in) long, but they are not used for feeding.

Filter Feeding

Three of the largest sharks—whale, basking, and megamouth sharks—use a different method of feeding. Although these sharks have hundreds of teeth, they are tiny and not suited to catching and killing prey. Instead, these sharks fill their immense mouth with ocean water containing tiny creatures. The creatures are filtered out and swallowed, while the water flows out through the shark's gills.

Life Cycle

Some female sharks give birth to live babies, known as pups, while others lay eggs. All shark mothers have one thing in common: They do not take care of their pups. Yet newborn pups can already swim and hunt, giving them the skills needed to survive.

Laying Eggs

Around a third of sharks lay eggs, which is known as oviparity (meaning "egg birth"). Egg-layers include bullhead sharks and some catsharks. Shark eggs have a tough case to protect the unborn baby, known as an embryo, as it develops. Egg cases are often called mermaid's purses. Eggs are often laid in rocky crevices or among coral or seagrass, to which the egg cases attach with long, threadlike tendrils.

A swell shark embryo is growing inside its egg case, which is around 10 cm (4 in) long.

Over time, the egg inside an egg case develops into an embryo.

A yolk sac contains food for the swell shark embryo.

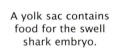

Great hammerhead pup

MOST LIVE PUPS

Whale shark: Litters of up to 300 live pups
Blue shark: Litters of up to 135 live pups
Tiger shark: Litters of up to 80 live pups
Great hammerhead: Litters of up to 55 live pups
Scalloped hammerhead: Litters of up to 40 live pups

The egg case will be home to the embryo for 9 to 12 months, after which it will break through the case using the extra-long dermal denticles on its back.

Lemon sharks are viviparous. Like a newborn human, a newborn lemon shark is still attached to its mother by a cord, through which it received food. The cord breaks as the pup swims away.

Live Pups

Female sharks give birth to live pups in one of two ways: viviparity or ovoviviparity. In viviparity (meaning "living birth"), babies develop inside their mother's body in a similar way to human babies. Viviparous sharks include hammerhead and requiem sharks. The majority of sharks are ovoviviparous. In ovoviviparity (meaning "egg living birth"), babies develop inside eggs, which hatch while they are still in the mother's body. The embryos continue to grow inside their mother until they are ready to be born, which can take up to 2 years. Mothers usually give birth to their pups in sheltered, shallow water.

DID YOU KNOW? Swell sharks are named for their ability to gulp in water when frightened, making themselves too big for a predator to swallow.

Together and Apart

Some sharks spend much of their time in a group, usually known as a school or shiver. Other sharks live alone, except when they gather to mate with other sharks of their species. Many sharks travel long distances to reach the same area for each mating season.

> In June and July, nurse sharks gather together to mate, returning to the same area every time.

Useful Schools

Many sharks spend time together and time apart. Great hammerheads swim in large schools during the day, but separate at night to hunt. Hunting alone means they do not compete for food. Small-spotted catsharks also hunt alone, but gather together to rest on the seafloor. This gives smaller sharks protection, as there are many eyes to watch for danger. Some sharks, including lemon sharks, do hunt together, helping each other to corner prey. Yet scientists have noticed that some sharks come together for no obvious reason, unless it is for company. Sand tigers are large predators that always return to the same shark "friends" after hunting trips.

Adult oceanic blacktip sharks are usually seen in schools. Pups form their own schools in the shallow waters where they are born.

AGGREGATIONS

Oceanic blacktip sharks: Up to 12,000
Basking sharks: Up to 1,400
Grey reef sharks: Up to 700
Whale sharks: Up to 400
Scalloped hammerheads: Up to 300

Grey reef shark aggregation

Migration and Aggregation

Although some sharks remain in the same area throughout their life, many sharks migrate (travel from one area to another) to reach suitable places to mate, give birth, or feed, gathering there in their tens or hundreds at certain times of year. These large, seasonal groups of sharks are known as aggregations. Some large, fast-swimming sharks, including dusky sharks, migrate to follow the migrations of the fish they prey on. Great white sharks are known to gather at particular beaches when they know that seal pups are born. Scientists believe that sharks know it is time to migrate from changes in water temperature.

Nurse sharks are found in warm, shallow water where mangroves grow.

This male and female shark are courting, or getting to know each other, before mating.

At certain times of year, whale sharks gather in coastal areas where there are plenty of fish eggs.

DID YOU KNOW? For 841 days, scientists tracked a female whale shark who swam a total of 20,142 km (12,516 miles) around the Pacific Ocean.

Extinct Sharks

The earliest sharks evolved around 420 million years ago, long before the first trees, flowers, dinosaurs, or monkeys. Like modern sharks, ancient sharks had cartilaginous skeletons, toothlike scales, and teeth that were replaced when they fell out.

Up to 20.3 m (67 ft) long, *Megalodon* (meaning "big tooth") was the largest shark ever known to exist. It lived between 23 and 3.6 million years ago.

Shark Fossils

Fossils tell us how ancient sharks looked. By studying features such as their tooth and fin shapes, we can make guesses about what and how they ate. Shark fossils formed when dead sharks sank to the water bottom and were buried quickly in sand or mud. The sharks' soft body parts, such as flesh and skin, usually rotted away. Over thousands of years, mineral-rich water seeped into the hard parts of the shark's body, slowly replacing the tooth or cartilage with minerals.

This rare fossil has preserved an image of the shark's whole body, as minerals in its skin and scales left behind a print on the rock.

Megalodon took in water through its mouth and soaked up oxygen using gills, before the water flowed out of five gill slits.

MEGALODON
Otodus megalodon
Mackerel shark

Length: 14 to 20.3 m (46 to 67 ft)
Range: Atlantic, Indian, and Pacific Oceans
Habitat: Tropical and temperate waters possibly to 1,000 m (3,280 ft) deep
Diet: Whales, seals, and sea turtles
Conservation: Extinct

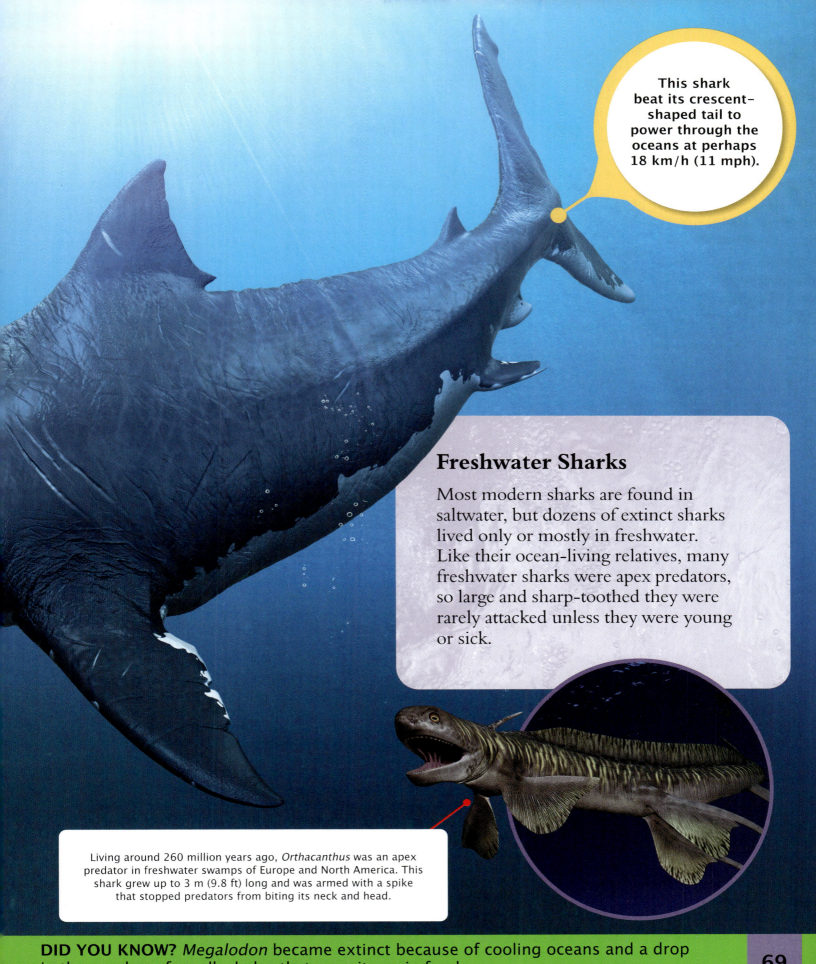

This shark beat its crescent-shaped tail to power through the oceans at perhaps 18 km/h (11 mph).

Freshwater Sharks

Most modern sharks are found in saltwater, but dozens of extinct sharks lived only or mostly in freshwater. Like their ocean-living relatives, many freshwater sharks were apex predators, so large and sharp-toothed they were rarely attacked unless they were young or sick.

Living around 260 million years ago, *Orthacanthus* was an apex predator in freshwater swamps of Europe and North America. This shark grew up to 3 m (9.8 ft) long and was armed with a spike that stopped predators from biting its neck and head.

DID YOU KNOW? *Megalodon* became extinct because of cooling oceans and a drop in the number of small whales that were its main food.

Under Threat

Around a third of shark species are threatened with extinction. To protect these wonderful fish, some countries have banned or limited shark fishing. There are now many sanctuaries where sharks and their habitats are protected from fishing and pollution.

Sharks in Trouble

Overfishing is the greatest threat faced by sharks. This is when too many fish in a species are caught, leaving the remaining fish unable to have enough babies to keep up their numbers. Sharks are particularly at risk because they do not mature enough to have babies until they are at least 4 years old. Sharks are fished for their meat; their fins, which are used in soup in some regions; and their cartilage and liver oil, which are used in cosmetics. In addition, sharks are often caught in nets and longlines (long cords with many hooks) meant for other fish. Another threat to sharks is water pollution by plastics and industrial chemicals. Construction along coastlines can also damage the shallow-water habitats where some shark pups live.

The oceanic whitetip is critically endangered due to fishing for its fins, meat, liver oil, and skin.

Sharks are sometimes fished for fun, known as sport fishing. However, this spinner shark was returned to the water unharmed. Spinner sharks are ranked as endangered.

DID YOU KNOW? Up to 100 million sharks are killed each year by humans fishing for money or sport.

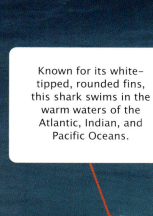

Known for its white-tipped, rounded fins, this shark swims in the warm waters of the Atlantic, Indian, and Pacific Oceans.

Conservation Status

The scientists of the International Union for Conservation of Nature count and monitor the world's animal species. They classify each species, such as great white shark or tiger shark, by how likely it is to become extinct in the near future:

The tawny nurse shark is ranked as vulnerable due to overfishing and damage to the seagrass meadows and coral reefs of its coastal habitat.

Critically endangered	At extremely high risk of becoming extinct.
Endangered	Very likely to become extinct in the near future.
Vulnerable	Facing a high risk of extinction in the medium term.
Near threatened	Likely to become endangered in the near future.
Least concern	Not currently at risk.

Female oceanic whitetips do not mature until 7 years old, then have only 5 or 6 pups every 2 years.

Sand tiger shark

MOST ENDANGERED
All critically endangered

Pondicherry shark: Coasts and rivers of southern Asia and Australasia
Ganges shark: Coasts and rivers of Bangladesh and India
Sawback angelshark: Coasts of western Africa and southern Europe
Daggernose shark: Coasts of northeastern South America
Sand tiger shark: Coasts of the Americas, Europe, Africa, Asia, and Australasia

Chapter 4: Shark Family Tree

Shark Orders

There are over 500 species of sharks, which scientists have divided into eight orders. The sharks in each order share characteristics. The largest order, with 270 species, is the ground sharks. The seven strange species of frilled and cow sharks make up the smallest order.

The great hammerhead is the largest species of hammerhead shark.

The great hammerhead shark is in the Sphyrnidae family of hammerhead sharks, in the ground shark order.

GREAT HAMMERHEAD SHARK

Sphyrna mokarran

Ground shark

Length: 3.5 to 6.1 m (11.5 to 20 ft)
Range: Atlantic, Indian, and Pacific Oceans
Habitat: Coastal tropical and temperate waters to 80 m (260 ft) deep
Diet: Crabs, squid, octopus, and fish including smaller sharks
Conservation: Critically endangered

Scientific Groups

Scientists divide animals into groups, based on how closely the animals are related. Animals in a group are similar in the way they look and behave because they evolved from the same ancestors. Orders are divided into families, which are split into genera, which are split into species. A species is a group of animals that look very alike, share habits, and can make babies together.

Shark Order	Scientific Name	Description	
Ground Sharks	*Carcharhiniformes*	The ground sharks have five gill slits, two dorsal fins, and an anal fin. Their wide, sharp-toothed mouths are located behind their eyes, when viewed from the side. Their eyes are protected by a third, see-through eyelid known as a nictitating membrane.	Silky shark
Carpet Sharks	*Orectolobiformes*	There are around 43 species of carpet sharks, which usually feed on the seabed. They have five gill slits, two dorsal fins, and an anal fin. When viewed from the side, their small mouth does not extend behind their eyes. Many have whisker-like sense organs known as barbels.	Nurse shark
Mackerel Sharks	*Lamniformes*	The 15 species of mackerel sharks have five gill slits, two dorsal fins, and an anal fin. Most species have a long snout and a large mouth that stretches behind their eyes. Most mackerel sharks are large.	Great white shark
Dogfish Sharks	*Squaliformes*	The 126 sharks in this order have five gill slits, two dorsal fins that are usually armed with spines, and no anal fin. They have a short mouth and a fairly pointed snout.	Spiny dogfish
Frilled and Cow Sharks	*Hexanchiformes*	These sharks have six or seven gill slits, one dorsal fin, and an anal fin. Their teeth are thornlike. Most sharks in this order live in cold, deep water. These sharks are similar to extinct sharks known only from fossils.	Broadnose sevengill shark
Bullhead Sharks	*Heterodontiformes*	This order contains nine species of small sharks. They have five gill slits, two dorsal fins armed with sharp spines, and an anal fin. Their mouth contains both sharp and flat teeth. Bullhead sharks feed at the ocean floor in tropical and subtropical oceans.	Port Jackson shark
Sawsharks	*Pristiophoriformes*	The eight species of sawsharks have long, sawlike snouts edged with sharp teeth. A pair of barbels is partway along the snout. Sawsharks have five or six gill slits, two dorsal fins, and no anal fin. These sharks usually live in coastal tropical waters.	Japanese sawshark
Angelsharks	*Squatiniformes*	There are around 24 species of angelsharks. They have five gill slits, two dorsal fins, and no anal fin. They have a flattened body and wide pectoral fins. Their jaws can be extended to give a rapid snap. Angelsharks usually live on sandy, shallow seabeds.	Pacific angelshark

DID YOU KNOW? Carpet sharks are named for their patterned bodies, which look a little like carpet designs.

GROUND SHARKS

Scalloped Hammerhead

Like other sharks in the hammerhead family, the scalloped hammerhead has an unusually shaped head, which is extended sideways into a hammer shape. The shark's eyes and nostrils are positioned at the tips of the hammer-like extension, which is known as a cephalofoil.

The front edge of this hammerhead's cephalofoil is scalloped, unlike that of the great hammerhead (see page 72), which is straighter.

There are 17 rows of small, sharp teeth on both the upper and lower jaw.

Helpful Hammer

This shark's head shape is useful for finding prey. Having eyes at either end of its cephalofoil enables the hammerhead to see above and below at all times. Although the shark does have a blind spot in front of its head, it swings its head from side to side as it swims to see what is directly ahead. In addition, the cephalofoil is covered in pores called ampullae of Lorenzini (see page 60), which detect the electrical charges given off by prey. This sense is called electroreception. Since the hammerhead's ampullae cover a wide area, it can even detect prey buried in sand.

SCALLOPED HAMMERHEAD

Sphyrna lewini

Ground shark

Length: 1.5 to 4.3 m (4.9 to 14 ft)
Range: Atlantic, Indian, and Pacific Oceans
Habitat: Coastal tropical and temperate waters to 500 m (1,600 ft) deep
Diet: Fish, squid, and octopus
Conservation: Critically endangered

Along with other sharks in the ground shark order, the scalloped hammerhead has five gill slits.

A school of scalloped hammerheads swims into deeper waters in search of food, but returns to shallower water to mate.

Swimming in a School

Scalloped hammerheads are usually seen in schools of up to several hundred sharks. Swimming in a group offers protection to younger sharks, which stay close to the surface while adults swim deeper. Attacks from larger sharks, such as great whites, will usually be made from below. In addition, scalloped hammerheads often work with members of their school to corner prey.

The black-tipped pectoral fins are held at an angle to help with balance.

DID YOU KNOW? A female scalloped hammerhead gives birth to litters of up to 40 live pups, but most do not survive to adulthood.

Bonnethead

Also known as a shovelhead, the bonnethead is a small member of the hammerhead shark family. It hunts by swinging its shovel-shaped head above the seafloor, trying to detect the tiny electrical charges given off by prey hiding among the mud and seagrass.

The Only Plant-Eater

The bonnethead is the only shark known to eat plants. It eats large amounts of seagrass, which may line its stomach for protection from the spiny shells of the blue crabs this shark also often eats. To crush these shells, the bonnethead has broad, flat teeth at the back of its mouth. It also has small, sharp teeth at the front of the mouth for grabbing little, slippery fish.

A bonnethead smells prey by detecting tiny particles—of blood, mucus, and other materials—that wash off prey and into its nostrils.

More than half a bonnethead's diet is made up of seagrass. Unlike other sharks, its guts make chemicals that can break down tough plant materials.

BONNETHEAD SHARK
Sphyrna tiburo
Ground shark

Length: 0.8 to 1.5 m (2.6 to 4.9 ft)
Range: Coasts of the Americas in the Atlantic and Pacific Oceans
Habitat: Seagrass beds of shallow bays in tropical and temperate waters to 80 m (260 ft) deep
Diet: Seagrass, blue crabs, shrimp, and small fish
Conservation: Endangered

DID YOU KNOW? A female bonnethead gives birth to live pups 5 months after mating, giving her the shortest known shark pregnancy.

This female bonnethead has a straight back to her cephalofoil, while a male bonnethead's cephalofoil has a bulging back.

Steering

Most hammerheads use their wide heads for steering as they swim, a little like a cyclist uses the handlebars to steer their bicycle. Other types of sharks use their pectoral fins for steering, but most hammerheads use them only for balance. The bonnethead has the smallest cephalofoil in the hammerhead family. Due to this small cephalofoil, the bonnethead has larger pectoral fins than other hammerheads and uses them energetically for making turns.

Bonnetheads turn and tilt their pectoral fins to swim up, down, left, and right.

77

Puffadder Shyshark

This small shark spends most of its time lying on the seafloor. Its narrow jaws have around 30 rows of teeth. Males, which prefer to eat worms, have long, three-pointed teeth for grasping. Females, which prey on tougher crabs and shrimp, have shorter, five-pointed teeth for crushing.

Being Shy

The puffadder is one of four species of shysharks. These sharks are named for their posture when they are frightened by a larger shark or other big fish. Shysharks curl into a circle and cover their eyes with their tail. This posture may help a shyshark look like a rock or piece of coral. It also makes the shark more difficult for a predator to swallow.

A pattern of white spots and orange "saddles" provides camouflage among rocks, sand, and coral.

This dark shyshark has curled into its defensive posture.

This puffadder shyshark is lying among Cape sea urchins and starfish in South Africa's False Bay.

DID YOU KNOW? The puffadder shyshark is named for the puff adder snake, which has a similar camouflage pattern.

PUFFADDER SHYSHARK

Haploblepharus edwardsii

Ground shark

Length: 48 to 69 cm (19 to 27 in)
Range: Coast of southern Africa in the Indian Ocean
Habitat: Sandy and rocky seafloors to 130 m (430 ft) deep
Diet: Crabs, shrimp, worms, and small fish
Conservation: Endangered

A puffadder shyshark's eyes are high on the sides of its head, enabling it to watch for danger nearly all around. Behind each eye is a hole known as a spiracle, through which water passes to the gills.

Its rounded pectoral fins and flattened body are suited to slow movement along the seafloor.

Cat Eyes

The shysharks are in the catshark family, in the ground shark order. Catsharks have wide, oval-shaped eyes that resemble a cat's. Their pupils (the holes through which light passes into the eye) are horizontal slits. While this shape would not be helpful for focussing on fast-moving prey, it is useful for watching for predators to the left and right. Like cats, catsharks have a see-through third eyelid, known as a nictitating membrane, that can close to protect the eyeball from damage.

Small-Spotted Catshark

This catshark has a slender body and a rounded snout. It is a slow swimmer that hunts for small prey at night, using stealth rather than speed. Like other catsharks, a female small-spotted catshark lays eggs rather than giving birth to live young.

A newborn small-spotted catshark pup is just 10 cm (4 in) long and must hide among the coral for protection.

Egg-Layer

A female lays up to 20 eggs in each mating season. The eggs are protected by a horny case that has curly stringlike tendrils. The female lays her eggs among coral or seaweed, often swimming round and round as she does so until the tendrils tangle on the fronds to stop the egg cases drifting away. The growing baby, known as an embryo, develops inside the egg case for between 5 and 11 months before hatching.

Inside this newly laid egg case is a yolk sac, which feeds the embryo as it grows.

SMALL-SPOTTED CATSHARK

Scyliorhinus canicula

Ground shark

Length: 0.6 to 1 m (2 to 3.3 ft)
Range: Coasts of Africa and Europe in the Atlantic Ocean
Habitat: Sandy, gravelly, and muddy seabeds to 400 m (1,300 ft) deep
Diet: Crabs, shrimp, fish, worms, and sea squirts
Conservation: Least concern

Researchers have noticed that some small-spotted catsharks prefer to be alone, which suggests that catsharks have different personalities.

Making Choices

This catshark spends the day resting on the seafloor, where it is well camouflaged by its pattern of dark brown spots on sandy skin. Scientists have noticed that some small-spotted catsharks prefer always to lie alone, relying on their own camouflage and stillness for safety. Other small-spotted catsharks always lie in a group, usually on top of each other, so they can share the work of looking out for predators.

A female small-spotted catshark deposited this egg case on a coral called a violescent sea-whip.

The egg case measures around 4 cm (1.6 in) long.

DID YOU KNOW? Young small-spotted catsharks stick prey to the spiky scales near their tail, then tear off bite-sized chunks.

Banded Houndshark

This species is named for the dark stripes along the backs of young banded houndsharks. These stripes fade with age. Banded houndsharks also change their diet as they get older, with young sharks eating shrimp and spoon worms but older sharks eating octopus and crab.

In and Out

Like other sharks, the banded houndshark has two nostrils, called nares, on the underside of its snout. Each nare has two openings, with water flowing in through one opening and out through the other. The banded houndshark has a flap in front of its nares, called a nasal flap, which directs the flow of water in and out of these openings. Inside the nare, the water runs over sensitive cells, which detect chemicals, or "smells," in the water then send signals to the shark's brain.

The banded houndshark has nasal flaps as well as long labial folds, which are furrows of skin around the corners of its mouth.

BANDED HOUNDSHARK

Triakis scyllium

Ground shark

Length: 1 to 1.5 m (3.3 to 5 ft)
Range: Coasts of Asia in the Pacific Ocean
Habitat: Sandy seabeds and seagrass beds in temperate waters to 150 m (490 ft) deep
Diet: Crabs, shrimp, octopus, worms, and fish
Conservation: Endangered

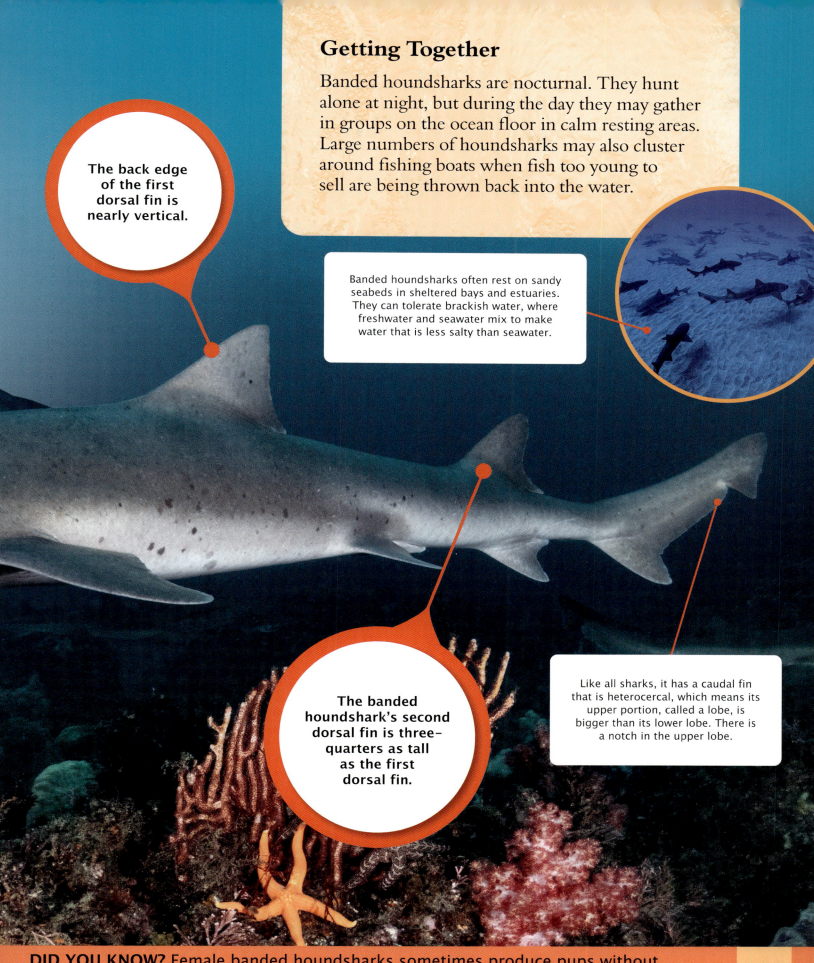

Getting Together

Banded houndsharks are nocturnal. They hunt alone at night, but during the day they may gather in groups on the ocean floor in calm resting areas. Large numbers of houndsharks may also cluster around fishing boats when fish too young to sell are being thrown back into the water.

The back edge of the first dorsal fin is nearly vertical.

Banded houndsharks often rest on sandy seabeds in sheltered bays and estuaries. They can tolerate brackish water, where freshwater and seawater mix to make water that is less salty than seawater.

The banded houndshark's second dorsal fin is three-quarters as tall as the first dorsal fin.

Like all sharks, it has a caudal fin that is heterocercal, which means its upper portion, called a lobe, is bigger than its lower lobe. There is a notch in the upper lobe.

DID YOU KNOW? Female banded houndsharks sometimes produce pups without mating with a male, which is an unusual ability known as parthenogenesis.

Caribbean Reef Shark

This shark is a member of the requiem shark family, in the ground shark order. Requiem sharks are fast and fearsome hunters. Yet Caribbean reef sharks are nicknamed "sleeping sharks" due to their habit of resting inside caves, usually where there are bubbling water currents to massage their skin.

All in the Name

The requiem sharks probably got their name from the French word for shark, *requin*. This word may have developed from the Latin word *requiem*, which means "death," as a result of many sharks' deadly hunting abilities. On the other hand, *requin* may have developed from the medieval French word *reschignier*, which means "to grimace with bared teeth."

A requiem shark's body is shaped like a torpedo (a fast-moving underwater weapon), which means it is long and bulky but slimmer at the snout and tail.

Like other requiem sharks, the Caribbean reef shark has a rounded snout and wide mouth.

DID YOU KNOW? Caribbean reef sharks can push their stomach out through their mouth, inside out, to get rid of parasites and food they cannot digest.

Balancing the Coral Reef

The Caribbean reef shark is the most common shark on the Caribbean Sea's Great Mayan Reef, which stretches along the coasts of Mexico, Belize, Guatemala, and Honduras in Central America. This shark is one of the largest predators on the coral reef, so it has a key role in maintaining the balance of reef life. By eating large numbers of smaller predators, such as yellowtail snappers, the shark prevents them from eating too many small, plant-eating animals. Plant-eaters keep the reef clear of algae, so the coral can survive.

The Great Mayan Reef is home to more than 60 species of hard corals, which are tiny animals that usually live in large groups called colonies. They build reefs by constructing hard skeletons around their soft bodies.

This shark is shy around humans but may bite divers if they block its path to prey.

If it feels threatened, this shark tries to frighten away predators by flapping its pectoral fins, arching its back, and darting in different directions.

CARIBBEAN REEF SHARK

Carcharhinus perezi

Ground shark

Length: 2 to 3 m (6.6 to 9.8 ft)
Range: Coasts of the Americas in the Atlantic Ocean
Habitat: Coral reefs in tropical waters to 30 m (98 ft) deep
Diet: Fish, octopus, squid, and crabs
Conservation: Endangered

85

Lemon Shark

This requiem shark is named for its yellow-brown skin, which camouflages the shark as it swims over the sandy seafloor. Lemon sharks live in groups, which work together to herd fish along the shoreline so they can be caught more easily.

Pick My Parasites

Lemon sharks hunt by night. During the day, they can often be seen resting on the seafloor. For a lemon shark, staying still takes a little more effort than moving, as—without water flow—it must suck water into its mouth and through its gills to take oxygen from it. However, a benefit to staying still is that fish named remoras can cling to the shark and feed on the irritating parasites that live on its skin. Parasites are small living things that live on or in other animals.

Remoras attach to a lemon shark by pressing their back to the shark's skin. A remora's flat, slatted dorsal fin acts like a sticky sucker.

LEMON SHARK

Negaprion brevirostris

Ground shark

Length: 2.4 to 3.1 m (7.9 to 10.2 ft)
Range: Coasts of the Americas and Africa in the Atlantic and Pacific Oceans
Habitat: Mangroves, river mouths, and bays in tropical and temperate waters to 90 m (295 ft) deep
Diet: Fish, crabs, crayfish, and seabirds
Conservation: Vulnerable

DID YOU KNOW? A lemon shark's large brain is as big in comparison to its body size as a bird's brain, which helps these clever sharks to work together.

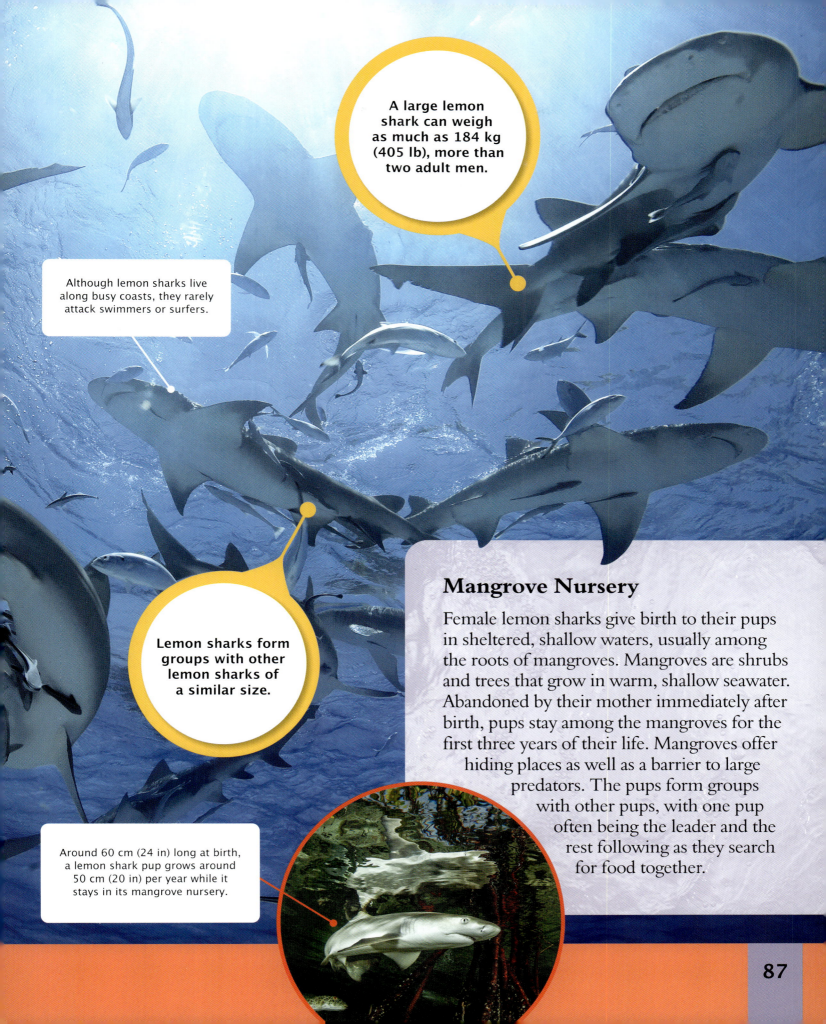

A large lemon shark can weigh as much as 184 kg (405 lb), more than two adult men.

Although lemon sharks live along busy coasts, they rarely attack swimmers or surfers.

Lemon sharks form groups with other lemon sharks of a similar size.

Around 60 cm (24 in) long at birth, a lemon shark pup grows around 50 cm (20 in) per year while it stays in its mangrove nursery.

Mangrove Nursery

Female lemon sharks give birth to their pups in sheltered, shallow waters, usually among the roots of mangroves. Mangroves are shrubs and trees that grow in warm, shallow seawater. Abandoned by their mother immediately after birth, pups stay among the mangroves for the first three years of their life. Mangroves offer hiding places as well as a barrier to large predators. The pups form groups with other pups, with one pup often being the leader and the rest following as they search for food together.

87

Bull Shark

Bull sharks are broader than most requiem sharks. They are named for their similarities to a bull: a stocky body, wide snout, and aggression. These dangerous sharks swim in shallow coastal water as well as in rivers, up to 1,100 km (700 miles) from the ocean.

Bull sharks are rarely seen together, except in late summer when they gather to mate in river mouths.

Attacks on People

Bull sharks are responsible for more attacks on people than any shark apart from the great white and tiger shark. This is partly because bull sharks are found in shallow coastal water where people swim and surf. Bull sharks are also territorial: They live alone and like to defend their area, or territory. Attacks on people are not usually deliberate, as bull sharks hunt in murky water and may bite a moving object simply to find out what it is.

Attacks by bull sharks are very rare. However, shark experts advise swimmers to punch an attacking shark hard in the eyes or gills to frighten it away.

BULL SHARK

Carcharhinus leucas

Ground shark

Length: 2 to 3.5 m (6.6 to 11.5 ft)
Range: Atlantic, Indian, and Pacific Oceans, and rivers in the Americas, Africa, Asia, and Australia
Habitat: Coasts in tropical and temperate waters to 150 m (490 ft) deep, as well as rivers and lakes
Diet: Turtles, birds, dolphins, and fish including other sharks
Conservation: Vulnerable

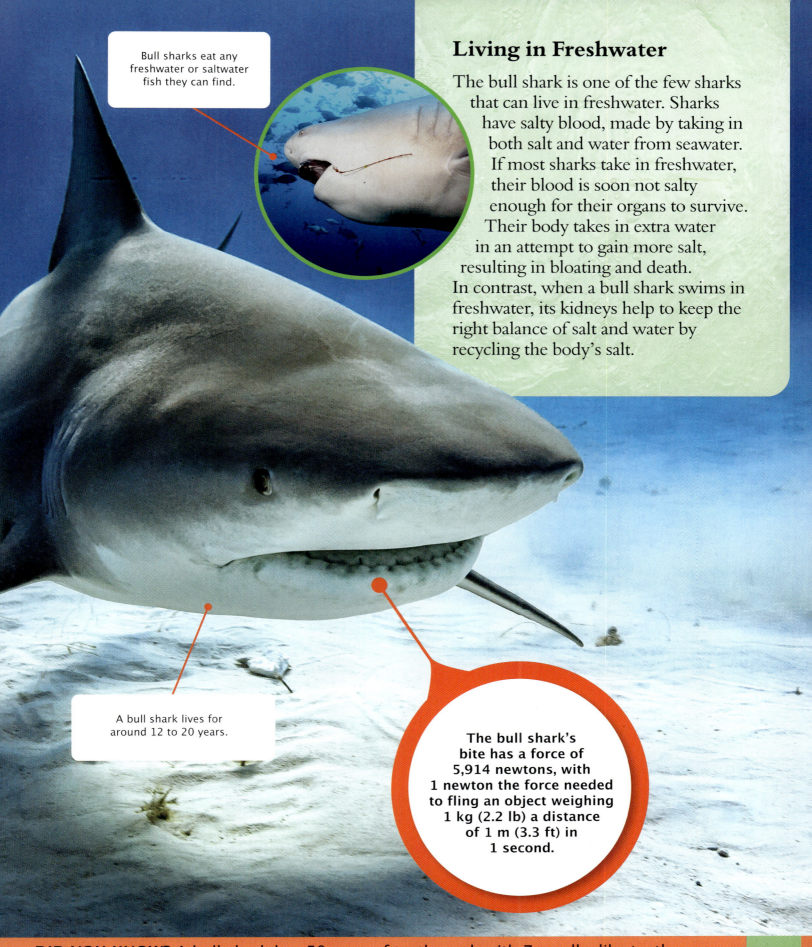

Bull sharks eat any freshwater or saltwater fish they can find.

Living in Freshwater

The bull shark is one of the few sharks that can live in freshwater. Sharks have salty blood, made by taking in both salt and water from seawater. If most sharks take in freshwater, their blood is soon not salty enough for their organs to survive. Their body takes in extra water in an attempt to gain more salt, resulting in bloating and death. In contrast, when a bull shark swims in freshwater, its kidneys help to keep the right balance of salt and water by recycling the body's salt.

A bull shark lives for around 12 to 20 years.

The bull shark's bite has a force of 5,914 newtons, with 1 newton the force needed to fling an object weighing 1 kg (2.2 lb) a distance of 1 m (3.3 ft) in 1 second.

DID YOU KNOW? A bull shark has 50 rows of teeth, each with 7 needle-like teeth, adding up to around 20,000 over the course of its life.

89

Tiger Shark

Up to 5.5 m (18 ft) long, the tiger shark is the longest of the requiem sharks. It is a fierce, solitary hunter, able to catch and eat a wider range of prey than any other shark, including hard-shelled sea turtles, fast-swimming dolphins, wriggling sea snakes—and other tiger sharks.

Eyelid for Safety

Like other ground sharks, the tiger shark has a see-through eyelid, known as a nictitating membrane, that can cover the eyeball for protection. When feeding, the shark closes the membrane and opens its jaws at exactly the same moment. The membrane is a thick body tissue covered in tiny scales. Like humans, a shark also has an upper and a lower eyelid, but these lids cannot close entirely over the eye.

The nictitating membrane moves over a tiger shark's eye from the bottom to the top.

The Laysan albatross is a common seabird across the North Pacific Ocean.

TIGER SHARK

Galeocerdo cuvier

Ground shark

Length: 3.3 to 5.5 m (10.8 to 18 ft)
Range: Atlantic, Indian, and Pacific Oceans
Habitat: Tropical and subtropical oceans to 900 m (3,000 ft) deep
Diet: Turtles, birds, dolphins, seals, sea snakes, crabs, and fish including other sharks
Conservation: Near threatened

Slanted for Slicing

A tiger shark's teeth are strong and sharp enough to break the shells of sea turtles, including those of leatherbacks, which reach 2 m (6.6 ft) long. This shark's teeth are short, only around 2.5 cm (1 in) long, but very wide. Each tooth has a slanting, knife-like tip for slicing through prey. On the left side of the mouth, these tips slant to the left, while on the right they slant to the right. This gives the shark extra grip while holding struggling prey. In addition, the tooth bases have jagged edges, which can saw through tough bones and shells.

A tiger shark has 48 slanted front teeth, which are replaced throughout its life.

The tiger shark swims slowly and stealthily toward prey, making a burst of speed at the final moment.

Inside a tiger shark's mouth are 10 openings through which water flows to its gills.

DID YOU KNOW? Tiger sharks will eat almost anything they find in the water, including human garbage such as wheels, bottles, nails, and balls.

Blacktip Reef Shark

This requiem shark can be identified by the black tips on its fins. Although the blacktip reef shark is timid with humans, it has been known to mistakenly nip the legs of people wading through the shallows of the Indian and Pacific Oceans.

Patrolling the Reef

An adult blacktip reef shark remains in one area of a coral reef for many years. This "home" area may be just 0.55 sq km (0.21 sq miles), among the smallest territories of any shark. The shark spends most of its time swimming backward and forward along the reef—until it finds prey. If a blacktip reef shark enters deeper water, it may fall victim to a tiger shark, so it usually remains on ledges of the reef, which offer protection from larger fish.

A blacktip reef shark patrols the edges and ledges of a coral reef through both the day and night.

BLACKTIP REEF SHARK

Carcharhinus melanopterus

Ground shark

Length: 1.5 to 1.8 m (5 to 6 ft)
Range: Coasts of Africa, Asia, and Australasia in the Indian and Pacific Oceans
Habitat: Tropical and subtropical waters to 80 m (260 ft) deep
Diet: Small fish, squid, octopus, and shrimp
Conservation: Vulnerable

DID YOU KNOW? At mating time, male and female blacktip reef sharks "court" each other by swimming one behind the other in curving, circling paths.

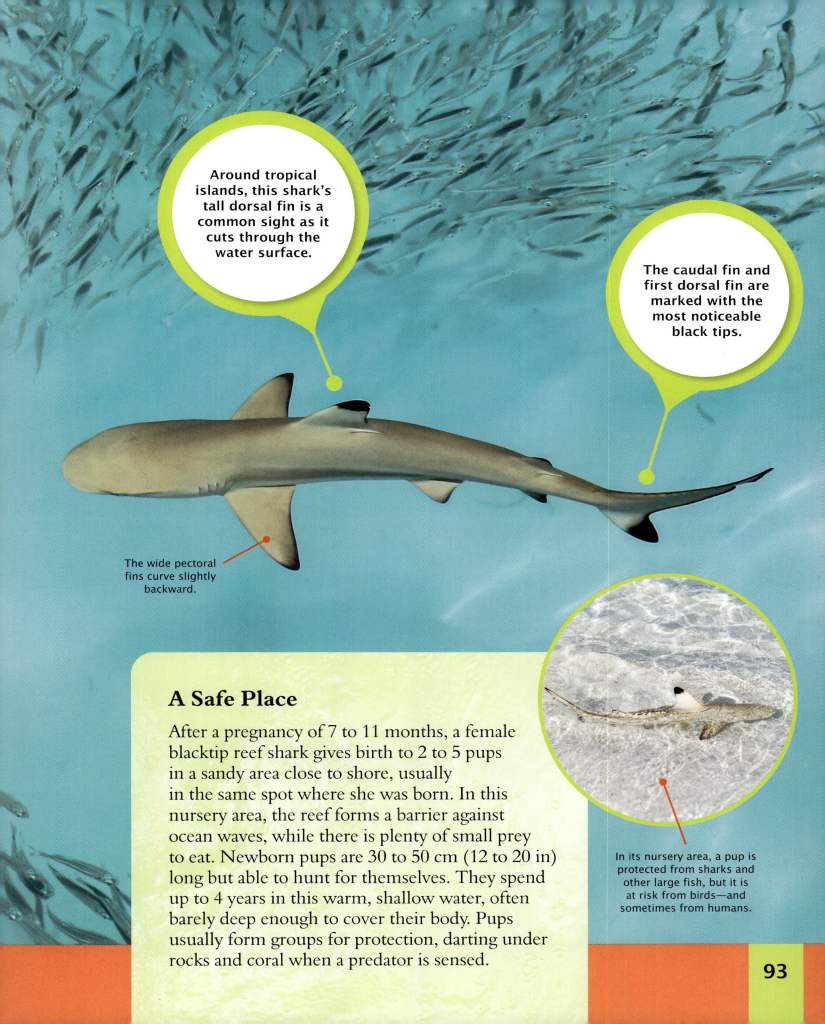

Around tropical islands, this shark's tall dorsal fin is a common sight as it cuts through the water surface.

The caudal fin and first dorsal fin are marked with the most noticeable black tips.

The wide pectoral fins curve slightly backward.

A Safe Place

After a pregnancy of 7 to 11 months, a female blacktip reef shark gives birth to 2 to 5 pups in a sandy area close to shore, usually in the same spot where she was born. In this nursery area, the reef forms a barrier against ocean waves, while there is plenty of small prey to eat. Newborn pups are 30 to 50 cm (12 to 20 in) long but able to hunt for themselves. They spend up to 4 years in this warm, shallow water, often barely deep enough to cover their body. Pups usually form groups for protection, darting under rocks and coral when a predator is sensed.

In its nursery area, a pup is protected from sharks and other large fish, but it is at risk from birds—and sometimes from humans.

93

CARPET SHARKS

Whale Shark

The largest of the sharks, the whale shark is harmless to humans —and to all animals larger than around a hand's width across. This shark feeds by filtering tiny creatures from the water. It is a slow swimmer, rarely moving faster than 5 km/h (3 miles per hour).

Tiny Food

Inside a whale shark's huge mouth are 300 rows of very small, useless teeth, which play no part in feeding. Instead, a whale shark has 20 sieve-like filter pads in front of its gills. Water can pass through the pads, but not tiny living things—such as eggs, small fish, and shrimp-like animals called krill—which the shark swallows. The whale shark can feed by swimming forward with its mouth open, so water and food flow inside, which is known as ram feeding. It can also feed by sucking water into its mouth, known as suction feeding.

A whale shark can weigh 15,000 kg (33,000 lb), more than 170 adult men.

A whale shark eats more than 20 kg (45 lb) of tiny living things every day.

WHALE SHARK

Rhincodon typus

Carpet shark

Length: 8 to 18.8 m (26 to 61.7 ft)
Range: Atlantic, Indian, and Pacific Oceans
Habitat: Tropical and temperate waters to 1,900 m (6,200 ft) deep
Diet: Eggs, krill, crab larvae, jellyfish, small fish, and squid
Conservation: Endangered

Huge Fish

The largest known whale sharks measure around 18.8 m (61.7 ft). Females grow more slowly than males but continue growing for much longer. The average female reaches around 14.5 m (48 ft) by the age of 50, which is when she is mature enough to mate. The average male grows to around 9 m (30 ft) long by the age of 30, which is when he is able to mate. Whale sharks are believed to live for between 80 and 130 years.

A whale shark's mouth is up to 1.55 m (5.1 ft) wide.

Like other carpet sharks, the whale shark has patterned dermal denticles.

For protection, the eyeballs are covered in dermal denticles and can also be pulled back into their sockets.

DID YOU KNOW? A whale shark can take in around 6,000 l (1,585 gallons) of water every hour—about 24,000 glasses.

Zebra Shark

During the day, this shark rests on the sandy seafloor between the corals of the reef where it lives. At night, the zebra shark uses its long, flexible body to squeeze into crevices in the reef, where it sucks up hiding prey using its muscly mouth.

Making Friends

Zebra sharks usually live alone, but come together to mate. Before mating, male and female zebra sharks court each other. The male may gently bite the female shark's tail. The pair swim side by side as the male holds on to the female's pectoral fin with his mouth. Female zebra sharks lay eggs, depositing up to 46 egg cases over a 112-day period.

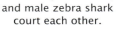
A female (at the front) and male zebra shark court each other.

Mature zebra sharks are spotted, while young zebra sharks are striped, a little like a zebra. This young shark's stripes are fading.

ZEBRA SHARK
Stegostoma tigrinum
Carpet shark

Length: 1.5 to 2.5 m (4.9 to 8.2 ft)
Range: Indian and Pacific Oceans
Habitat: Coral reefs in tropical waters to 60 m (200 ft) deep
Diet: Shellfish, shrimp, small fish, and sea snakes
Conservation: Endangered

DID YOU KNOW? Scientists think the stripes of young zebra sharks make them look like venomous sea snakes, which helps to keep predators away.

Larger than the zebra shark's eye, the spiracle is used for sucking in water when the shark is resting so it can continue to take oxygen.

Swimming Style

This shark's caudal (tail) fin is nearly as long as the rest of its body. Unlike more solid-bodied and short-tailed sharks, such as great whites, the zebra shark swims by making snake-like wiggles of its tail and body. This shark has five deep ridges running along its body, which help water wash quickly over the shark so it is not bashed against coral or rocks by choppy waves.

Each nostril has a barbel, a sense organ that helps with tasting and smelling prey.

In most sharks, tall dorsal fins help with stability, but the zebra shark has low dorsal fins. However, it has deep body ridges and wide pectoral fins to help with balance.

97

Blind Shark

This shark lives in shallow water close to shore. It is sometimes left stranded in rock pools when the tide goes out. Unusually for a shark, the blind shark can survive up to 18 hours out of water by switching off the brain and body functions that are not essential.

Not Blind

Despite its name, this shark has good eyesight. It got its name from its habit of pulling its eyeballs back into their sockets and shutting its thick lower eyelids if caught by a fisherman. This protects its eyes from injury and from drying out in the air. The blind shark is a night-time hunter. Like many other nocturnal sharks, it makes up for poor visibility by having barbels that help it taste and smell prey.

The blind shark has a very long barbel projecting from each nostril.

Hiding in a Cave

During the day, blind sharks usually hide in small caves or under ledges. If surprised by a human or a predator—such as a larger shark—the blind shark becomes completely motionless or tries to wriggle further into its hiding place.

The blind shark likes rocky habitats with plenty of shelter.

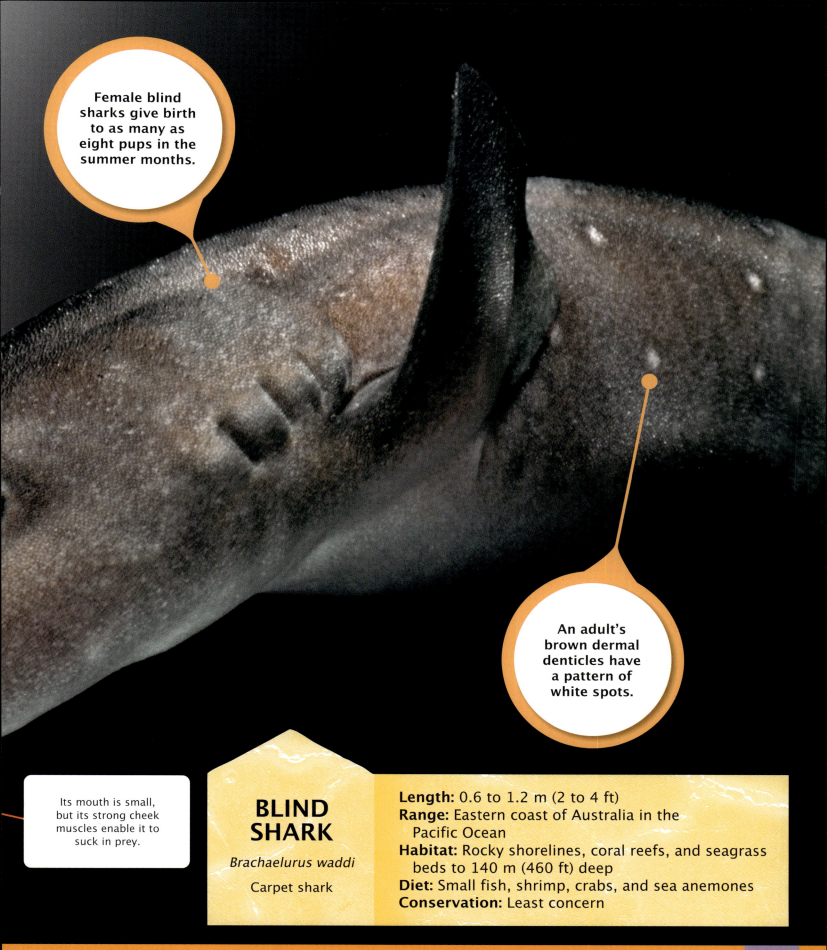

Female blind sharks give birth to as many as eight pups in the summer months.

An adult's brown dermal denticles have a pattern of white spots.

Its mouth is small, but its strong cheek muscles enable it to suck in prey.

BLIND SHARK

Brachaelurus waddi

Carpet shark

Length: 0.6 to 1.2 m (2 to 4 ft)
Range: Eastern coast of Australia in the Pacific Ocean
Habitat: Rocky shorelines, coral reefs, and seagrass beds to 140 m (460 ft) deep
Diet: Small fish, shrimp, crabs, and sea anemones
Conservation: Least concern

DID YOU KNOW? If provoked by a diver, the blind shark can bite then cling hard to their skin with its powerful sucking mouth, making it hard to remove.

Nurse Shark

At night, the nurse shark hunts alone, searching among the sand and mud for small, resting creatures. During the day, this shark lies on the seafloor with its school. No one is sure how it got the name "nurse," but it may be related to the fact that females give birth to live pups.

Suck and Spit

Nurse sharks have a small mouth that creates extremely powerful suction to catch prey. To suck in prey, the shark opens its mouth quickly. Water rushes in to fill the empty space in the jaws, drawing prey with it. If prey is too large, the shark breaks it apart by shaking its head vigorously as it sucks. It also uses a suck and spit action: spitting prey out and sucking it back in again and again until it is torn apart.

The nurse shark's small mouth makes its sucking action very focussed and accurate.

A nurse shark school stays in one small area of coastline, where it has its own preferred resting place.

Slow but Snappy

The nurse shark is slow moving and spends much of the day lying still, along with up to 40 others. This "sleepiness" has led foolish divers to approach the shark, thinking it is harmless. When bothered by a human, this shark will bite, putting it among the top 20 shark species most likely to attack humans. This shark's small teeth mean its bites are not life-threatening.

DID YOU KNOW? The nurse shark preys on sea snails by flipping over their shell then sucking out their soft body.

NURSE SHARK

Ginglymostoma cirratum

Carpet shark

Length: 2.1 to 3 m (6.9 to 9.8 ft)
Range: Coasts of the Americas and Africa in the Atlantic and Pacific Oceans
Habitat: Coral reefs and rocky areas in tropical and subtropical waters to 75 m (246 ft) deep
Diet: Fish, octopus, squid, lobsters, sea urchins, clams, and snails
Conservation: Vulnerable

These nurse sharks are swimming among staghorn, fire, and elkhorn corals off the coast of Belize, in Central America.

The nurse shark's two dorsal fins are rounded, with the first located above the pelvic fins.

Its snout is broad and rounded. Inside the mouth are many small, notched teeth for crushing hard-shelled prey.

101

Brownbanded Bamboo Shark

This long-bodied shark is often found on the sheltered, muddy seafloor between coral reefs and the shore. It hunts at night, by nosing into mud, sand, crevices, and rock pools while using its sensitive barbels to find small creatures.

The brownbanded bamboo shark is listed as near threatened due to fishing, pollution, and damage to its coral reef habitat.

Changing Patterns

Young bamboo sharks have dark-brown bands running around their pale-brown body, earning this species its name. These bands help to camouflage pups, which spend the day hiding among the dappled light and shadows around seagrass, rocks, and coral. The bands fade as the sharks reach maturity, leaving adults a uniform light brown that serves as good camouflage on the seafloor.

Its short barbels help with tasting and smelling prey that is hidden under mud or sand.

A young brownbanded bamboo shark hides from predators such as lemon sharks and killer whales.

BROWNBANDED BAMBOO SHARK

Chiloscyllium punctatum

Carpet shark

Length: 0.8 to 1.3 m (2.6 to 4.3 ft)
Range: Coasts of Asia and Australasia in the Indian and Pacific Oceans
Habitat: Muddy seafloors in tropical and subtropical waters to 85 m (279 ft) deep
Diet: Small fish, shrimp, crabs, and worms
Conservation: Near threatened

Bamboo Sharks

This shark is in the bamboo shark family, also known as longtail carpet sharks. They are named for their long body and extremely lengthy tail, which make them look a little like a bamboo stem. Bamboo sharks have two dorsal fins positioned far back on their body, with the first dorsal fin over their pelvic fin. All bamboo sharks live on the seafloor in shallow waters of the Indian and Pacific Oceans.

Bamboo sharks have pupils that narrow to vertical slits. This type of pupil is useful in the constantly changing light of shallow water as it enables the pupil to narrow quickly in sudden sunlight to moderate the amount of light entering the eye.

Parasites (which live in or on other living things) are found in this shark's gills, where they feed on blood and mucus.

DID YOU KNOW? When this shark bites hard-shelled prey, its small, sharp teeth fold backward so they can crush the shell with their strong, flat fronts.

Epaulette Shark

> This shark can survive for 2 hours out of water, by increasing the blood supply to its brain to keep it fed with oxygen.

This member of the bamboo shark family takes its name from the white-edged, dark spot behind each pectoral fin. These spots look rather like the shoulder ornaments, known as epaulettes, that are sometimes worn by soldiers.

Its large nostrils, or nares, are nearly at the tip of its snout.

Walking Along

Like other members of its family, the epaulette shark lives on the sandy, muddy, or rocky seafloor. Rather than swimming along, it often "walks" across the bottom. It does this by wriggling its body and pushing off the floor with its paddle-shaped pectoral and pelvic fins. This means the shark can move through water too shallow for swimming. It is even able to walk out of the water to reach isolated rock pools where it can find many small, trapped creatures.

The epaulette shark's pectoral and pelvic fins are broad, muscly, and capable of wider movements than those of most other sharks.

A Frightening Eye

This shark's white-and-black epaulette is known as an eyespot, a marking that resembles an eye. This type of marking is found in animals from butterflies to birds. The eyespot may frighten away predators as it seems to be a huge eye that belongs to a much bigger animal. The marking may also distract predators into attacking the shark's side rather than its sensitive and vital head.

This shark's predators include fish such as larger sharks and groupers.

EPAULETTE SHARK

Hemiscyllium ocellatum

Carpet shark

Length: 0.7 to 1 m (2.3 to 3.3 ft)
Range: Coasts of New Guinea and Australia in the Indian and Pacific Oceans
Habitat: Coral reefs and rock pools in tropical waters to 50 m (160 ft) deep
Diet: Worms, crabs, small fish, and shrimp
Conservation: Least concern

Like many sharks that live on the seafloor, the epaulette shark has eyes positioned near the top of its head so it can look upward.

DID YOU KNOW? Unlike most sharks, the epaulette shark sometimes chews food for up to 10 minutes so it can crush shells and bones.

Indonesian Speckled Shark

This little-known shark is found only in one small region, around the coasts and islands of West Papua, in Indonesia. Like other bamboo sharks, its body and fin shapes are suited to slow swimming and crawling along the seafloor and into holes in rocks and reefs.

> Diamond-shaped, extra-thick dermal denticles do not help this shark swim faster but do give protection as it rubs against rough coral and rocks.

Bamboo Eggs

Like other bamboo sharks, this shark is an egg-layer. After a female bamboo shark has reached around the age of seven, she lays a pair of eggs every couple of weeks during the mating season. She produces around 50 eggs in a year, always laying them among the shadows under overhanging coral. The babies spend 4 to 5 months developing inside their egg case before hatching. Pups are less than 19 cm (7.5 in) long at birth.

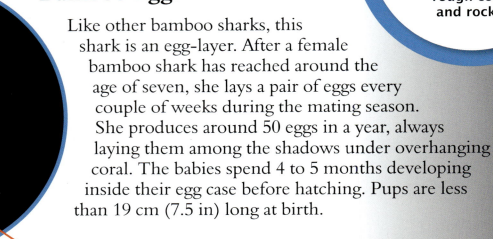

About 10 cm (4 in) long, the egg case of a bamboo shark is very strong. Like the egg cases of other sharks, it is made of strands of collagen, a material also found in human cartilage, bones, and skin.

INDONESIAN SPECKLED CARPET SHARK

Hemiscyllium freycineti

Carpet shark

Length: 37 to 72 cm (15 to 28 in)
Range: Coasts of western New Guinea in the Pacific Ocean
Habitat: Coral reefs, rock pools, and seagrass meadows in tropical waters to 12 m (39 ft) deep
Diet: Worms, crabs, shrimp, and small fish
Conservation: Near threatened

DID YOU KNOW? This shark's scientific name, *Hemiscyllium freycineti*, means "half-dogfish of Freycinet," after the 19th-century explorer who first studied it.

Humans have a white coating to their eye, known as the sclera, but a shark's sclera is protected by a thick body tissue containing cartilage.

Like other members of its family, the Indonesian speckled carpet shark has a large spiracle.

During the day, the Indonesian speckled carpet shark hides in crevices on the coral reef.

Shallow Habitat

This shark lives in shallow, near-shore habitats, where its speckled dermal denticles are effective camouflage, helping to break up the shark's outline as it lies among the dappled light and waving plants. Yet its habitats are under threat from fishing practices such as using dynamite to create explosions that kill both fish and coral.

Tasselled Wobbegong

This shark belongs to the wobbegong family of well-camouflaged carpet sharks, which spend most of their time lying on the seafloor or coral. "Wobbegong" comes from Aboriginal Australian words that may mean "shaggy beard," due to these sharks' tassel-like skin flaps.

Tasty Tassels

This wobbegong has a fringe of branching skin flaps that runs from its snout to its pectoral fins. Looking like seaweed or coral, these flaps camouflage the wobbegong while also attracting small prey to feed on them. When prey animals try to take a nibble, the wobbegong sucks them into its wide mouth, then pierces them with its needle-like teeth. The skin flaps also have sensitive cells that help the wobbegong smell and taste prey.

The tasselled wobbegong is usually an ambush predator, lying in wait for prey then making a sudden, deadly movement.

The wobbegong's flattened, patterned body keeps it camouflaged on the coral reef so unsuspecting prey swims near.

TASSELLED WOBBEGONG

Eucrossorhinus dasypogon

Carpet shark

Length: 1.2 to 1.8 m (3.9 to 5.9 ft)
Range: Coasts of New Guinea and northern Australia in the Indian and Pacific Oceans
Habitat: Coral reefs in tropical waters to 50 m (160 ft) deep
Diet: Fish, squid, shrimp, octopus, and squid
Conservation: Least concern

DID YOU KNOW? The tasselled wobbegong kills sharks almost as big as itself, including brownbanded bamboo sharks.

Fishy Tail

While the tasselled wobbegong waits for prey, it often waves its tail back and forth over its own head, making a slow movement like a small, swimming fish. The tail is also shaped rather like a fish, complete with a dark eyespot at its base. When larger fish approach to snatch the supposed fish, they are caught by the wobbegong instead.

When waving its tail, the wobbegong rests with its head tilted upward, putting its mouth within sucking distance of any animal that takes the bait.

While resting during the daytime, this shark will seize prey that comes near, but it does move in search of food at night.

The shark uses its broad, curved pectoral fins for pulling itself over the reef.

109

Ornate Wobbegong

This shark is named for its busy, lace-like pattern of golden brown, cream, and blue-beige. Its underside is yellowish green. This gorgeous pattern provides good camouflage among the corals and seaweeds of the ornate wobbegong's coral reef home.

Mega Mouth

Wobbegongs suck in prey by shooting forward their jaws while expanding their throat and mouth with powerful muscles. Water and prey are sucked in to fill the huge empty space in the mouth. Small prey is swallowed without chewing. If wobbegongs catch an animal too large to swallow, they hold it in their jaws until it dies from exhaustion or lack of oxygen, then bite off chunks with their long, sharp teeth.

The heavy pattern breaks up the shark's outline into irregular shapes that blend with coral and rocks.

Bumps above the shark's eyes keep them hidden in shadow so they do not attract attention.

An ornate wobbegong can open its mouth wide enough to prey on fish as large as a green moray, which reaches 2.5 m (8.2 ft) long when fully grown.

ORNATE WOBBEGONG

Orectolobus ornatus

Carpet shark

Length: 1.7 to 2.9 m (5.6 to 9.5 ft)
Range: Eastern coast of Australia in the Pacific Ocean
Habitat: Coral reefs and algae-covered seafloor in tropical to temperate waters to 100 m (330 ft) deep
Diet: Fish, crabs, lobsters, and octopus
Conservation: Least concern

Looking Up

Like other wobbegongs, the ornate wobbegong has eyes positioned at the top of its head, which lets this bottom-dweller get a wide view of approaching prey and predators. Unlike most sharks, which do not have fully closing eyelids, wobbegongs have more moveable upper and lower eyelids that cover the eyeballs when the shark is pressing its snout into sand or coral in search of prey.

The tissue surrounding the ornate wobbegong's pupil, known as the sclera, is yellow. This helps the shark maintain camouflage.

Like other wobbegongs, this shark has two dorsal fins on the back half of its body, behind its pelvic fins.

DID YOU KNOW? This shark is known to lie in rock pools, where it can give painful bites to humans who accidentally step too close.

Necklace Carpet Shark

A member of the collared carpet shark family, this shark is named for the dark, necklace-like patch that lies behind its eyes. Entirely harmless to humans, this small shark has a long, slim body.

Hiding Away

The necklace carpet shark spends its days hidden in caves or on the seafloor, where it shelters from predators among coral, kelp, and seagrass. At night, it uses its barbels and electroreception (see page 60) to smell and sense the movements of small creatures that are hiding among the coral or in the sand.

This shark can be told apart from other members of its family by the small, pale spots on its collar and the large, dark spots on its pectoral fins.

Seafloor Mimic

Scientists think that collared carpet sharks can change the shade of their skin to better match the seafloor on which they are lying. The change takes several minutes, with the shark becoming darker, lighter, or more blotchy. These changes are triggered by the shark's brain releasing a hormone (a chemical that carries messages) which causes melanophores in the skin to expand or contract. Melanophores are cells that are filled with a dark pigment, named melanin.

The necklace carpet shark's dark collar helps with camouflage by breaking up the shark's outline.

NECKLACE CARPET SHARK

Parascyllium variolatum

Carpet shark

Length: 60 to 91 cm (24 to 36 in)
Range: Southern coast of Australia in the Indian and Pacific Oceans
Habitat: Coral reefs, kelp forest, and seagrass meadows in temperate waters to 180 m (590 ft) deep
Diet: Prawns, shrimp, and crabs
Conservation: Least concern

This shark's pupils narrow to horizontal slits, a shape that gives a wide field of vision and is useful for watching out for predators.

The necklace carpet shark's collar may help other members of its species to recognize it at mating time.

A pair of barbels is used for smelling and tasting prey.

DID YOU KNOW? Two unknown species of collared carpet sharks have been found since the start of the 21st century: the ginger and elongate carpet sharks.

MACKEREL SHARKS

Great White Shark

Reaching 6.1 m (20 ft) long, this feared hunter is the world's largest predatory fish. It is responsible for more bites to humans than any other shark. The great white is in the order of mackerel sharks, which are known for their large mouth and wide-opening jaws.

Apex Predator

The great white shark is an apex predator (or "top hunter"), which means that—unless it is young or sick—it is rarely preyed on by other animals. With its powerful, smoothly shaped body and strong jaws, a great white can attack prey as big as a killer whale. Although the great white usually hunts alone, it may work with other members of its school, which can include two or more sharks. When attacking, a great white swims slowly closer to its prey, then makes a sudden rush at up to 24 km/h (15 miles per hour).

A great white has up to 300 jagged-edged, triangular teeth in seven rows. When teeth in the front row break, the teeth behind move forward.

The great white shark's first dorsal fin is large and triangular.

GREAT WHITE SHARK

Carcharodon carcharias

Mackerel shark

Length: 3.4 to 6.1 m (11 to 20 ft)
Range: Atlantic, Indian, and Pacific Oceans
Habitat: Coastal and offshore waters to 1,200 m (3,900 ft) deep
Diet: Fish, dolphins, whales, seals, sea lions, sea turtles, and seabirds
Conservation: Vulnerable

Clever Camouflage

A great white's underside is white, but its back is dark. This pattern is a form of camouflage known as countershading. Such shading makes it difficult for prey swimming at the water surface to see a great white as it moves through the dark water below. Yet for prey swimming below a great white, the shark's pale belly makes it hard to spot against the sunlight shining down through the water.

Like all mackerel sharks, a great white has five gill slits.

A great white shark's most powerful sense is smell: It can smell a drop of blood in 10 billion drops of water.

Great whites attack prey on the water surface by making a sudden upward rush, launching both shark and prey out of the water.

DID YOU KNOW? At the moment when it attacks prey, a great white's eyeballs roll backward in their sockets for protection.

Shortfin Mako Shark

A close relative of the great white shark, the shortfin mako is the fastest known shark. Its smoothly shaped, muscly body and pointed snout let it cut through the water at high speed, reaching 74 km/h (46 miles per hour) in the moments before it seizes prey.

Nicely Named

In the Māori language of New Zealand, mako means "shark" or "shark tooth." In the past, Māori craftspeople carved necklaces from shark teeth, which were believed to give the wearer the strength and ferocity of a shark. The mako is also known as the blue pointer, due to the metallic blue of its back. This shade makes the shark blend with the water, when viewed from above. Yet the shark's underside is white, so that—when seen from below—it is difficult to spot when sunlight is shining down through the water.

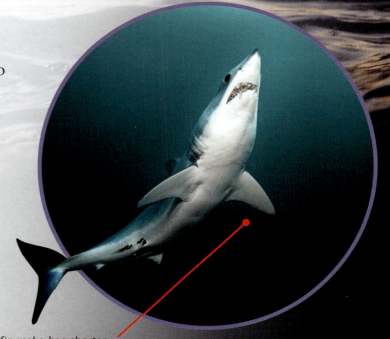

The shortfin mako has shorter pectoral fins than its close relative, the longfin mako shark.

SHORTFIN MAKO SHARK

Isurus oxyrinchus

Mackerel shark

Length: 3 to 4 m (9.8 to 13 ft)
Range: Atlantic, Indian, and Pacific Oceans
Habitat: Open ocean in tropical and temperate waters to 150 m (490 ft) deep
Diet: Fish, octopus, squid, porpoises, turtles, and birds
Conservation: Endangered

DID YOU KNOW? The shortfin mako has the strongest recorded bite of any shark, inflicting the same force as a weight of 1,360 kg (3,000 lb).

When prey such as porpoises or sharks is too large to swallow, the shortfin mako bites chunks out of them.

Hooked Teeth

The shortfin mako shark has very sharp, pointed teeth up to 2 cm (0.8 in) long. The teeth are curved into a hook shape. Such teeth are ideal for piercing and holding on to large, fast-swimming fish, such as tuna, swordfish, and other sharks. Tuna are among the quickest fish, reaching speeds of up to 75 km/h (47 miles per hour). After this shark grasps fish, they are swallowed whole, then digested in the mako's stomach for around 2 days.

The shortfin mako shark has extremely large eyes that help it see during deep-water dives.

This shark is a lone hunter, swimming up to 2,000 km (1,240 miles) a month as it follows schools of fish.

The shortfin mako shark usually rests near the water surface at night.

117

Porbeagle

The porbeagle spends part of its time alone and part with its school, when it has been seen chasing other members of its group in play. That makes this intelligent fish one of the few sharks that is known to play.

This shark's first dorsal fin and pectoral fins are large, but it has very small second dorsal, anal, and pelvic fins.

Watching the Porbeagle

The porbeagle is ranked as vulnerable due to decades of overfishing. Today, many countries have banned or limited the catching of porbeagles. Conservationists monitor this shark's numbers and movements so that more controls can be put in place if needed. Sharks are fitted with telemetry (meaning "distant measuring") tags that record their location, depth, speed, and temperature. The information is sent as radio waves or sound waves to a satellite or underwater receiver, from which it is transmitted to a conservationist's computer.

Captured off the Canadian coast, this porbeagle is being measured and tagged before being released unharmed back into the water. If the shark is caught again, it will be remeasured to discover its growth.

The porbeagle has 26 to 29 front teeth in its lower jaw, with wide gaps between each tooth.

118

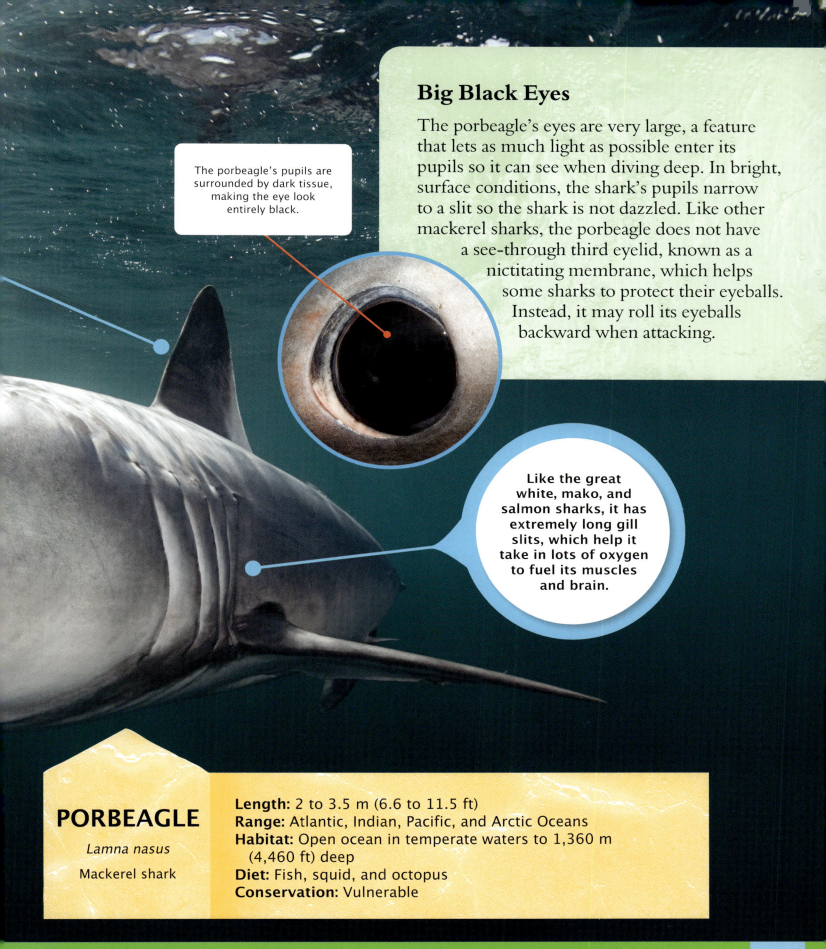

Big Black Eyes

The porbeagle's eyes are very large, a feature that lets as much light as possible enter its pupils so it can see when diving deep. In bright, surface conditions, the shark's pupils narrow to a slit so the shark is not dazzled. Like other mackerel sharks, the porbeagle does not have a see-through third eyelid, known as a nictitating membrane, which helps some sharks to protect their eyeballs. Instead, it may roll its eyeballs backward when attacking.

The porbeagle's pupils are surrounded by dark tissue, making the eye look entirely black.

Like the great white, mako, and salmon sharks, it has extremely long gill slits, which help it take in lots of oxygen to fuel its muscles and brain.

PORBEAGLE

Lamna nasus

Mackerel shark

Length: 2 to 3.5 m (6.6 to 11.5 ft)
Range: Atlantic, Indian, Pacific, and Arctic Oceans
Habitat: Open ocean in temperate waters to 1,360 m (4,460 ft) deep
Diet: Fish, squid, and octopus
Conservation: Vulnerable

DID YOU KNOW? Porbeagles give birth to live pups, which feed on unused eggs while they grow inside their mother, a practice known as oophagy ("egg-eating").

Salmon Shark

The majority of sharks live in warm water, but the salmon shark lives in the cool North Pacific Ocean. For most of the year, male and female salmon sharks swim in separate groups, with females usually in the northeastern Pacific and most males in the northwestern Pacific.

Salmon-Eater

The salmon shark is named for its main prey: salmon. From July to September, these sharks gather in a large aggregation in Alaska's Prince William Sound. Here they catch salmon that are migrating from the ocean to the rivers where they lay their eggs. In addition, salmon sharks eat other large fish, such as cod, herring, and sablefish, as well as most prey they can fit in their mouth.

Scientists estimate that, every year, salmon sharks catch between 76 and 146 million salmon in Prince William Sound.

Warm-Blooded

Most sharks, like most fish, are cold-blooded, which means the temperature of their body is the same as the water around them. Five species of closely related mackerel sharks—the salmon, great white, shortfin mako, longfin mako, and porbeagle sharks—are warm-blooded. This means they can raise their body temperature above the temperature of the surrounding water. They can do this thanks to a complex system of blood vessels, which keeps the heat given off by their muscles as they work. In addition, these sharks' higher body heat keeps their muscles warm. Warmer muscles are able to move faster, giving them an advantage over the cold-blooded fish they prey on.

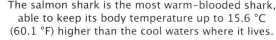

The salmon shark is the most warm-blooded shark, able to keep its body temperature up to 15.6 °C (60.1 °F) higher than the cool waters where it lives.

SALMON SHARK

Lamna ditropis

Mackerel shark

Length: 2 to 3 m (6.6 to 9.8 ft)
Range: North Pacific Ocean
Habitat: Temperate and polar waters to 668 m (2,192 ft) deep
Diet: Fish, sea otters, and birds
Conservation: Least concern

Copepod parasites are trailing from this shark's first dorsal fin, where they feed on skin and blood.

This salmon shark is cruising in Alaska's Prince William Sound, in the northwestern United States.

Its eyes are positioned toward the front of its head, so the two eyes can work together to judge the distance to fleeing prey.

DID YOU KNOW? The average salmon shark eats around 5 kg (11 lb) of food every day, about the weight of a 2-month-old baby.

Sand Tiger Shark

This shark is named for its habit of hunting in shallow water, often among the breaking waves on sandy beaches. The sand tiger hunts at night, sometimes feeding on large schools of fish alongside other members of its group.

This species can be recognized by the reddish spots on its upper side.

Gulping Air

Sharks are heavier than water, so they sink slowly if they do not swim (see page 58). The sand tiger has a unique answer to this problem: It swims to the surface and gulps air into its stomach, which has the same effect as putting on an air-filled float vest. This habit lets the sand tiger float in the water without moving or making a noise. It is able to surprise passing fish, snatching them up with a sudden sideways snap.

A sand tiger kills prey up to half its own length, using its long, sharp teeth to bite prey into three or four easy-to-swallow chunks.

SAND TIGER SHARK

Carcharias taurus

Mackerel shark

Length: 2 to 3.2 m (6.6 to 10.5 ft)
Range: Atlantic, Indian, and Pacific Oceans
Habitat: Sandy coasts and coral reefs in tropical and temperate waters to 190 m (623 ft) deep
Diet: Fish including small sharks
Conservation: Critically endangered

DID YOU KNOW? This overfished shark is critically endangered due to mothers having only two pups at a time, in every second or third year.

The sand tiger has a long, cone-shaped snout.

It usually swims with its mouth open, revealing its curving teeth—and earning itself the alternative name of "spotted ragged-tooth shark."

This female sand tiger is pregnant.

Cannibal Babies

Female sand tigers give birth to live pups. Females have two areas, called horns, in their uterus. The uterus is a stretchy organ where unborn babies, known as embryos, develop. At the start of a pregnancy, each horn has up to 50 embryos. When one of the embryos reaches 10 cm (4 in) long, it eats all the smaller embryos in its horn. This practice, known as embryophagy (meaning "embryo-eating"), ensures that only large, strong pups are born. The two remaining embryos then eat any unused eggs. After a pregnancy of 8 to 9 months, the mother gives birth to two pups around 1 m (3.3 ft) long.

Smalltooth Sand Tiger Shark

Little is known about the habits of this rarely seen shark, which spends most of its time in rocky, deep-water habitats. It has been seen around ridges and mountains on the ocean floor, as well as hydrothermal vents, where water heated inside the Earth bubbles up.

Small Teeth

The smalltooth sand tiger looks similar to the sand tiger shark, although it is not much more closely related to it than to other mackerel sharks. The smalltooth has smaller teeth than its lookalike. While the sand tiger has sharp front teeth suited to cutting and broader back teeth suited to crushing, the smalltooth's teeth are all alike. This suggests it eats smaller, easier-to-chew prey.

The smalltooth sand tiger has 48 to 56 front teeth in its upper jaw and 36 to 46 front teeth in its lower jaw.

Shark Gods

The smalltooth sand tiger can be spotted around Pacific Islands, where sharks are important characters in myths. For many centuries, people on these islands lived by fishing aboard small boats, with sharks both the most prized catch and the most feared danger. In Hawaiian mythology, Kamohoali'i was a shark god, believed to help ships lost at sea by shaking his tail in front of the ship and then leading the way home.

In Fiji, the shark god Dakuwaqa protected fishermen at sea. The god could take any form he liked, but was often carved as a fierce-looking warrior.

Despite the smalltooth sand tiger's size and fierce appearance, it is gentle toward divers.

The caudal fin has a much larger upper lobe than lower lobe, making it highly asymmetrical.

The large, triangular anal fin is almost the same size as the second dorsal fin.

SMALLTOOTH SAND TIGER SHARK

Odontaspis ferox

Mackerel shark

Length: 3.6 to 4.5 m (11.8 to 14.8 ft)
Range: Atlantic, Indian, and Pacific Oceans
Habitat: Rocky seafloors, coral reefs, and sandy coasts in tropical waters to 2,000 m (6,562 ft) deep
Diet: Fish, squid, and shrimp
Conservation: Vulnerable

DID YOU KNOW? When frightened, this shark stops, opens its mouth, turns around, then shakes its tail toward the threat.

Megamouth Shark

Like the basking and whale sharks, the megamouth is a filter feeder. It eats small animals that it filters from the water by swimming with its mouth open or by sucking in water. Tiny animals are caught on sieve-like bristles in its mouth, while the water flows out of its gills.

Up and Down

The megamouth follows the daily movements of the zooplankton (tiny animals) that it eats. During the day, the shark swims in the murky depths. As night falls, zooplankton including shrimp and krill swim from the depths to the surface to feed on phytoplankton in the safety of darkness. Phytoplankton are tiny, plantlike living things that float near the surface, where they make their own food from sunlight during the day. The megamouth swims upward with the shrimp and krill, spending the night at a depth of around 12 to 25 m (39 to 82 ft).

The megamouth's daily movement between upper and lower waters is known as a diel vertical migration (diel means "daily").

As its name suggests, the megamouth shark has a huge mouth, up to 1.3 m (4.3 ft) wide, so it can take in big mouthfuls of water.

DID YOU KNOW? Since the megamouth shark was discovered in 1976, only around 100 of these rare sharks have been spotted.

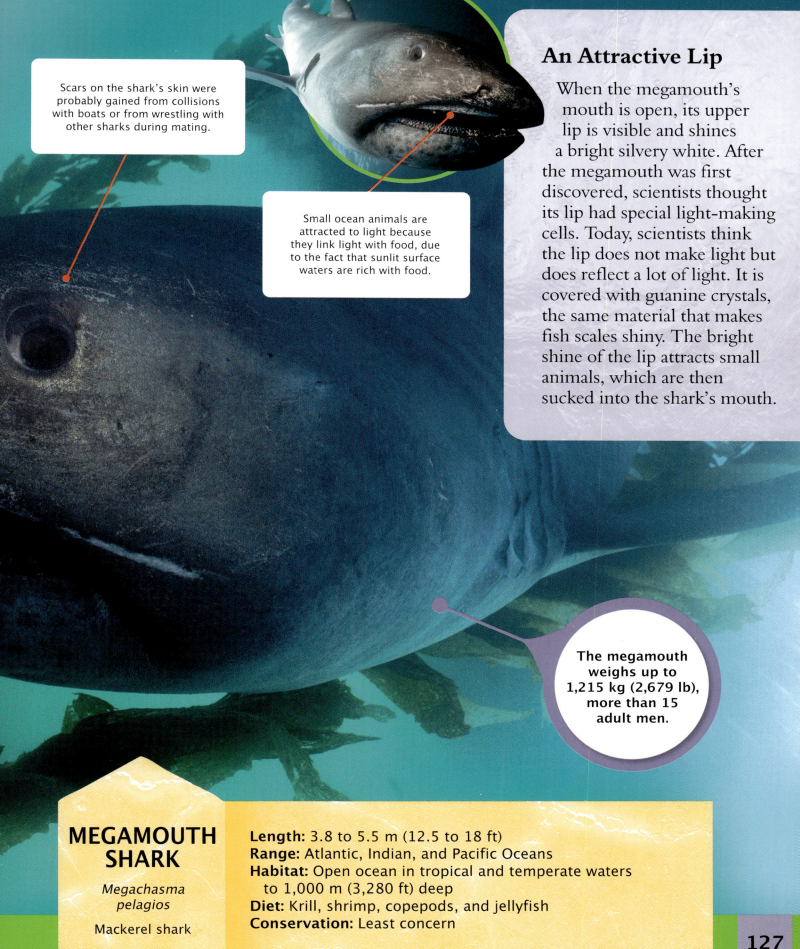

Scars on the shark's skin were probably gained from collisions with boats or from wrestling with other sharks during mating.

Small ocean animals are attracted to light because they link light with food, due to the fact that sunlit surface waters are rich with food.

An Attractive Lip

When the megamouth's mouth is open, its upper lip is visible and shines a bright silvery white. After the megamouth was first discovered, scientists thought its lip had special light-making cells. Today, scientists think the lip does not make light but does reflect a lot of light. It is covered with guanine crystals, the same material that makes fish scales shiny. The bright shine of the lip attracts small animals, which are then sucked into the shark's mouth.

The megamouth weighs up to 1,215 kg (2,679 lb), more than 15 adult men.

MEGAMOUTH SHARK

Megachasma pelagios

Mackerel shark

Length: 3.8 to 5.5 m (12.5 to 18 ft)
Range: Atlantic, Indian, and Pacific Oceans
Habitat: Open ocean in tropical and temperate waters to 1,000 m (3,280 ft) deep
Diet: Krill, shrimp, copepods, and jellyfish
Conservation: Least concern

Basking Shark

This filter feeder is the second largest shark, after the whale shark. It is named for its habit of swimming near the zooplankton-filled water surface, giving the mistaken idea that it is basking—or warming itself in the sunshine.

A Simple Life

Of all the sharks, the basking shark has the lightest brain compared to its body weight. Little brain power is needed for this shark's slow and simple lifestyle. Unlike the megamouth and whale sharks, this shark never sucks water into its mouth, but only feeds by swimming with its mouth open, at around 3.7 km/h (2.3 miles per hour). Due to the basking shark's great size, it has little need to use brain power for escaping from predators.

It has 1,500 teeth, each around 0.5 cm (0.2 in) long, which are not used for feeding but are "leftovers" from long-ago ancestors that did bite prey.

On each side of the basking shark's mouth are five openings to its gills, known as gill arches. Each arch is lined with dark, bristly gill rakers that stop tiny animals from entering the gills—directing them toward the shark's throat instead. The gill rakers become so worn with use that they are shed and regrown around once a year.

BASKING SHARK

Cetorhinus maximus

Mackerel shark

Length: 7 to 12.3 m (23 to 40.3 ft)
Range: Atlantic, Indian, Pacific, and Arctic Oceans
Habitat: Temperate and polar waters to 910 m (2,990 ft) deep
Diet: Copepods, fish eggs, and worms
Conservation: Endangered

This basking shark is feeding around St Michael's Mount, in England's Cornwall.

Every 2 to 3 minutes, the basking shark flutters its gills to shake trapped food from its gill rakers.

Giant Gills

The basking shark's gill slits nearly encircle its head, making them the largest slits of any shark. These huge openings let around 1,360,000 l (360,000 gallons) of water pass through the gills every hour. To ensure this water contains enough zooplankton to power the basking shark's giant body, these sharks migrate across the ocean to find areas where weather and currents combine to create clouds of zooplankton.

The basking shark usually swims alone, but in summer may gather in aggregations of up to 1,400 in water that is thick with zooplankton.

DID YOU KNOW? A quarter of this shark's weight is its immense liver, which is filled with lighter-than-water oil and helps the shark float with little effort.

Pelagic Thresher

Like other members of the thresher shark family, this shark has a caudal (tail) fin with an exceptionally long upper lobe. Measuring up to 1.5 m (4.9 ft), the tail makes up nearly half the shark's length. The upper lobe is shaped like a thresher, a curved farming tool used to cut crops.

Thrashing Tail

The pelagic thresher hunts in the ocean's twilight zone, around 200 m (660 ft) below the surface, where there is little sunlight. When this shark finds a school of small fish, it circles them to drive the fish into a ball. Then the shark swims swiftly toward the ball, swinging its tail forward over its head so the fish are whipped by the long upper lobe. The slapped, stunned fish are easily snapped up in the shark's jaws.

The pelagic thresher has around 21 small, sharp front teeth in both its upper and lower jaws, with between 5 and 11 rows of replacement teeth behind.

This shark's smoothly shaped body and powerful tail enable it to swim at well over 30 km/h (18 miles per hour).

The pelagic thresher uses its tail as a deadly weapon.

DID YOU KNOW? Pelagic means "living in the open ocean" and comes from the ancient Greek word for wide ocean far from land.

Overfishing

The pelagic thresher is endangered due to overfishing for its meat, fins, skin, and oil. It is also popular with sport fishermen due to its exciting speed and its habit of leaping out of the water, flicking its tail to push itself higher. The shark may jump from the water, known as breaching, to knock parasites off its skin as it slaps back down.

Its large, round eyes help this shark to see prey in deep, dim water.

As well as being fished deliberately, the pelagic thresher is caught accidentally in longlines and nets, often trapped by its own long tail.

PELAGIC THRESHER

Alopias pelagicus

Mackerel shark

Length: 2.6 to 4.3 m (8.5 to 14 ft)
Range: Indian and Pacific Oceans
Habitat: Open ocean in tropical waters to 250 m (820 ft) deep
Diet: Fish, shrimp, and squid
Conservation: Endangered

Goblin Shark

This strange, deep-water shark is extremely rare, although it is not considered endangered because it is not often caught in nets. The goblin shark lives in coastal waters but swims near the ocean floor, so it is never spotted by swimmers.

Its skin has a pinkish tint due to being quite see-through, letting us see blood vessels beneath the skin.

Scary Snout

The goblin shark is named for its long, flat snout, which looks like the long nose of a nasty, monstrous creature in a fairy tale. Some scientists have wondered if the shark uses its snout to stir up the mud and sand of the seafloor to find small prey, but others think the snout is too soft for this use. However, the snout is covered in many ampullae of Lorenzini (see page 60), which can detect the tiny electric fields given off by prey as they move.

The body is not well muscled, making this shark a slow swimmer that must creep up on prey, then use its speedy jaw for surprise.

The goblin shark's snout is used to detect the movement of small creatures in the dark water or hiding in the sand.

132

GOBLIN SHARK

Mitsukurina owstoni

Mackerel shark

Length: 3 to 6 m (9.8 to 19.7 ft)
Range: Atlantic, Indian, and Pacific Oceans
Habitat: Coastal tropical and temperate waters to 1,370 m (4,490 ft) deep
Diet: Fish, squid, and shrimp
Conservation: Least concern

The goblin shark's jaws spring forward at up to 3.14 m/s (10.3 ft per second). The shark has nail-like teeth with 35 to 53 front teeth in the upper jaw and 31 to 62 front teeth in the lower jaw.

Catapulting Jaw

When the goblin shark finds prey, it shoots its jaws forward and upward. At other times, the jaws are held back by stretchy tissues named ligaments. When the shark relaxes these ligaments, the effect is like releasing the elastic on a catapult. At the same time, the floor of the shark's mouth drops, expanding the space in the mouth so that water and prey are sucked inside.

The fins are small and soft, preventing this shark from making quick changes of direction.

DID YOU KNOW? Discovered near Japan in 1898, the goblin shark is named *tenguzame* in Japanese, after the *tengu*, a mythical creature with a long nose.

DOGFISH SHARKS

Greenland Shark

The largest shark in the dogfish shark order, the Greenland shark can weigh over 1,400 kg (3,100 lb). It is also the longest-living of all sharks, able to survive for over 270 years and possibly as many as 500 years.

Cold and Slow

The Greenland shark is the only shark that can live in Arctic waters year round, swimming in water between -2 and 7 °C (28.4 and 44.6 °F). Like most sharks, its body cannot warm itself, so its temperature matches the cold water. A cold body works more slowly, so the shark's heart beats only once every 12 seconds. This shark also moves very slowly, with an average speed of only 1.22 km/h (0.76 miles per hour). Scientists think the shark's slow-working body is linked with its extremely long life.

A parasite named *Ommatokoita* is attached to this shark's eye. Almost blinded, the shark must rely on its excellent senses of smell and hearing.

The Greenland shark waits near holes in the Arctic sea ice to catch seals that are coming up for air.

DID YOU KNOW? Growing by only 0.5 to 1 cm (0.2 to 0.4 in) a year, Greenland sharks do not mature enough to have babies until they are around 150 years old.

Kæstur hákarl is dried in the open air. Around 100 Greenland sharks are caught deliberately every year, while around 3,500 more are caught accidentally in nets meant for fish such as halibut.

Poisonous Flesh

The Greenland shark's flesh contains the chemical trimethylamine oxide, which is made by the shark's body to stabilize its processes in the extremely cold and often deep water where it lives. This chemical also makes the shark poisonous, but in Iceland its flesh is a traditional delicacy known as *kæstur hákarl*. To make the flesh safe to eat, it is buried in the ground for 6 to 12 weeks to press out the trimethylamine oxide, then hung in strips to dry for several months.

With its small pectoral fins, this shark is a slow swimmer which often feeds on prey that is sleeping or already dead.

These scars were made by bumping against rocks while searching for food and by fighting with other sharks over territory or mates.

GREENLAND SHARK

Somniosus microcephalus

Dogfish shark

Length: 2.4 to 6.4 m (7.9 to 21 ft)
Range: North Atlantic and Arctic Oceans
Habitat: Temperate and Arctic waters to 2,200 m (7,200 ft) deep
Diet: Fish, squid, and seals
Conservation: Vulnerable

135

Velvet Belly Lanternshark

This small shark is named "velvet belly" for its black underside, which is a different shade from the brown of the rest of the shark's body. Like most dogfish sharks, it has sharp spines on its two dorsal fins, which it uses to defend itself against predators by arching its back.

Lantern of Light

Found in deep, dark water, the 45 species of lanternsharks are named for their ability to make light. The velvet belly lanternshark's belly and sides are dotted with light-making organs known as photophores. When the shark is seen from below, the blue-green lights make it almost invisible against faint sunlight. This form of camouflage is known as counterillumination.

This lanternshark has five pairs of very short gill slits.

The velvet belly's dorsal spines are lit up by its photophores, which is a warning to predators—such as larger sharks and the longnosed skate—that it has weapons and will defend itself.

VELVET BELLY LANTERNSHARK

Etmopterus spinax

Dogfish shark

Length: 40 to 60 cm (16 to 24 in)
Range: Northeastern Atlantic Ocean
Habitat: Tropical and temperate waters to 2,490 m (8,170 ft) deep
Diet: Shrimp, krill, squid, fish, and worms
Conservation: Vulnerable

The long, curved spine on this shark's second dorsal fin is twice as long as the first dorsal fin's spine.

Like other dogfish sharks, the velvet belly lanternshark has no anal fin.

Holding and Cutting

Each small tooth in the velvet belly's upper jaw has up to six cusps (points). These teeth are used for gripping prey. The teeth in the lower jaw are much bigger and squarer. Arranged so they overlap, these bottom teeth form a cutting blade like the edge of a saw. The shark slices flesh using a circular movement of the lower jaw, while the upper jaw holds prey still.

On average, a velvet belly lanternshark has 31 front teeth in its lower jaw and 24 in its upper jaw.

DID YOU KNOW? All velvet belly lanternsharks have the same, particular pattern of lights along their sides, which helps them spot each other at mating time.

Angular Roughshark

Like the four other species of roughsharks, the angular roughshark has extremely rough skin. Its tall, sharp-spined dorsal fins are often caught in fishing nets, leading to this small shark being ranked as endangered.

With its forward-pointing defensive spine, the angular (meaning "sharp cornered") first dorsal fin earns the shark its name.

Shaped for Slowness

Roughsharks have an unusual body shape, flattened and broad at the underside and narrow at the top, making them almost triangular when viewed from the front. For swimming fast, a smoothly shaped, torpedo-like body (narrow at the snout and tail) is ideal for cutting through open water. In contrast, a roughshark's body shape is suited to slow swimming and to hovering over the seafloor as it watches for prey. The shark's flattened underside is ideal for resting on the seafloor for long periods.

A closely related roughshark, the prickly dogfish has tall, sail-like dorsal fins, with the first dorsal fin rising from just behind its eyes.

ANGULAR ROUGHSHARK

Oxynotus centrina

Dogfish shark

Length: 0.5 to 1.5 m (1.6 to 4.9 ft)
Range: Eastern Atlantic Ocean
Habitat: Muddy and algae-covered seafloors in tropical and temperate waters to 660 m (2,170 ft) deep
Diet: Worms, shrimp, fish, and shark eggs
Conservation: Endangered

In this close-up of the sailfin roughshark's skin, we can see that each dermal denticle has four sharp cusps (points): two central, backward-pointing cusps, with a smaller cusp on each side.

Rough Skin

All sharks have rough skin, but the roughsharks have skin with particularly prickly dermal denticles. These help to protect these small sharks from attack. If predators, such as larger sharks, manage to avoid a roughshark's dorsal spines, they will find themselves deeply scraped by the large, knife-like dermal denticles that cover its body.

This shark has such large nostrils, called nares, that scientists think it relies on its sense of smell for detecting prey hiding on the seafloor.

Its pale, fleshy lips are covered in bumps, called papillae, which may contain sensitive cells that help with touching, smelling, and tasting prey.

DID YOU KNOW? The angular roughshark feeds on the contents of shark egg cases, including eggs laid by its own species.

Spiny Dogfish

The spiny dogfish is named for its two sharp spines, one at the front of each dorsal fin. This shark and some of its close relatives in the dogfish shark family are among the only sharks that are venomous.

Venomous Spines

The spiny dogfish makes mild venom, a liquid that causes pain when injected into predators. The venom is produced in glands at the base of the dogfish's spines, so it coats their sharp tips. If the shark is attacked, it curls up, arches its back, and jabs its spines into the predator. This makes most attackers swim away fast. Humans pricked by spiny dogfish report swelling and a burning feeling around the wound.

Dogfish take their name from their habit of hunting in doglike packs, with some packs including over a thousand sharks.

SPINY DOGFISH

Squalus acanthias

Dogfish shark

Length: 0.8 to 1.6 m (2.6 to 5.2 ft)
Range: Atlantic, Indian, Pacific, and Arctic Oceans
Habitat: Temperate and subarctic waters to 700 m (2,300 ft) deep
Diet: Squid, jellyfish, worms, fish, crabs, and shrimp
Conservation: Vulnerable

DID YOU KNOW? Newborn spiny dogfish pups are so aggressive they will attack fish two to three times their size.

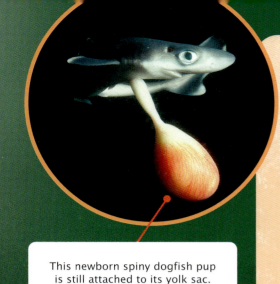

This newborn spiny dogfish pup is still attached to its yolk sac.

Longest Pregnancy

This shark has the longest known pregnancy of any shark: 22 to 24 months. The spiny dogfish is ovoviviparous, which means that unborn babies, named embryos, develop inside eggs that remain inside their mother's body. After mating, a shell grows around the fertilized eggs to protect them. After 4 to 6 months, the egg shells are shed but the embryos stay inside their mother, feeding on an attached ball of food, known as a yolk sac. After nearly 2 years, up to 11 pups are born head first, with a sheath covering their spines so the mother is not injured.

This species can be recognized by the small white spots along its back and flanks.

The spiny dogfish usually hunts close to the seafloor.

The shark is countershaded to escape the notice of prey and predators: Its underside is white, while its back and flanks are brown.

141

Cookiecutter Shark

This shark was named for its habit of biting round chunks of flesh out of large prey, leaving a mark that looks as if it was made by a cookie cutter. These wounds are around 5 cm (2 in) across and 7 cm (2.8 in) deep.

Cookie Bites

Although this shark swallows small prey whole, it takes round bites out of large prey. Its large, triangular bottom teeth form a jagged, saw-like cutting blade. In addition, its lips are large, fleshy, and hardened with cartilage. To take a bite, this shark clamps onto large prey by sucking, forming a tight seal with its lips. Then it bites, using its narrow upper teeth as anchors while it turns its body to make a circular cut. At the same time, this shark vibrates its jaw, creating a movement like an electric carving knife.

Cookiecutter bites can be seen on ocean animals such as humpback whales (pictured), as well as on submarines and underwater cables.

With its small dorsal and pectoral fins, this shark is not a fast swimmer, so it hovers while watching for passing prey.

The caudal fin is beaten from side to side when the shark needs a brief burst of speed to attach itself to prey.

DID YOU KNOW? The cookiecutter loses its lower teeth regularly, then swallows them so their tough calcium can be recycled into new teeth.

COOKIECUTTER SHARK

Isistius brasiliensis

Dogfish shark

Length: 42 to 56 cm (17 to 22 in)
Range: Atlantic, Indian, and Pacific Oceans
Habitat: Around islands in tropical and temperate waters to 3,505 m (11,500 ft) deep
Diet: Bites from whales, dolphins, seals, and fish, as well as whole squid
Conservation: Least concern

Not lit by photophores, this dark collar looks like a small fish when seen from below—and may attract hungry prey within reach of the cookiecutter's jaws.

Making Light

As with other sharks in its kitefin family, the skin of the cookiecutter's belly contains thousands of light-making organs named photophores. These hold tiny lenses and pigments to brighten and tint the light. The photophores make light by mixing together two chemicals made by the shark, creating a chemical reaction (a permanent change) that releases light energy. The ability to make light is known as bioluminescence.

Another member of the kitefin family, the pygmy shark is also bioluminescent. Most kitefins live in the ocean's twilight zone, 200 to 1,000 m (660 to 3,300 ft) below the surface. The water is dimly lit during the day, when the shark's blue light makes it hard to spot. Yet, in total darkness, the shark's light attracts prey.

143

FRILLED AND COW SHARKS

Broadnose Sevengill Shark

This shark is in the Hexanchiformes order of frilled and cow sharks, which have one, spineless dorsal fin and six or seven pairs of gill slits. These are the most primitive sharks: Sharks that looked like modern frilled and cow sharks lived at least 160 million years ago.

Cow Sharks

The broadnose sevengill is one of five living species of cow sharks. With its cow shark relative the sharpnose sevengill, it shares the record for the shark with most gill slits. Only sharks in the Hexanchiformes order and the sixgill sawsharks have more than five pairs of gill slits. The cow sharks are named for their usually round, blunt snouts, which make them look a little like cows. They have wide, comb-shaped teeth in their lower jaw, for tearing prey, and sharp, jagged teeth in their upper jaw, for holding wriggling prey.

Like other cow sharks, the broadnose sevengill has only one, small dorsal fin, as well as a caudal fin with a much larger upper than lower lobe.

BROADNOSE SEVENGILL SHARK

Notorynchus cepedianus

Frilled and cow shark

Length: 1.5 to 3 m (4.9 to 9.8 ft)
Range: Atlantic, Indian, and Pacific Oceans
Habitat: Coastal tropical and temperate waters to 1,870 ft (570 m) deep
Diet: Fish, seals, crabs, snails, and octopus
Conservation: Vulnerable

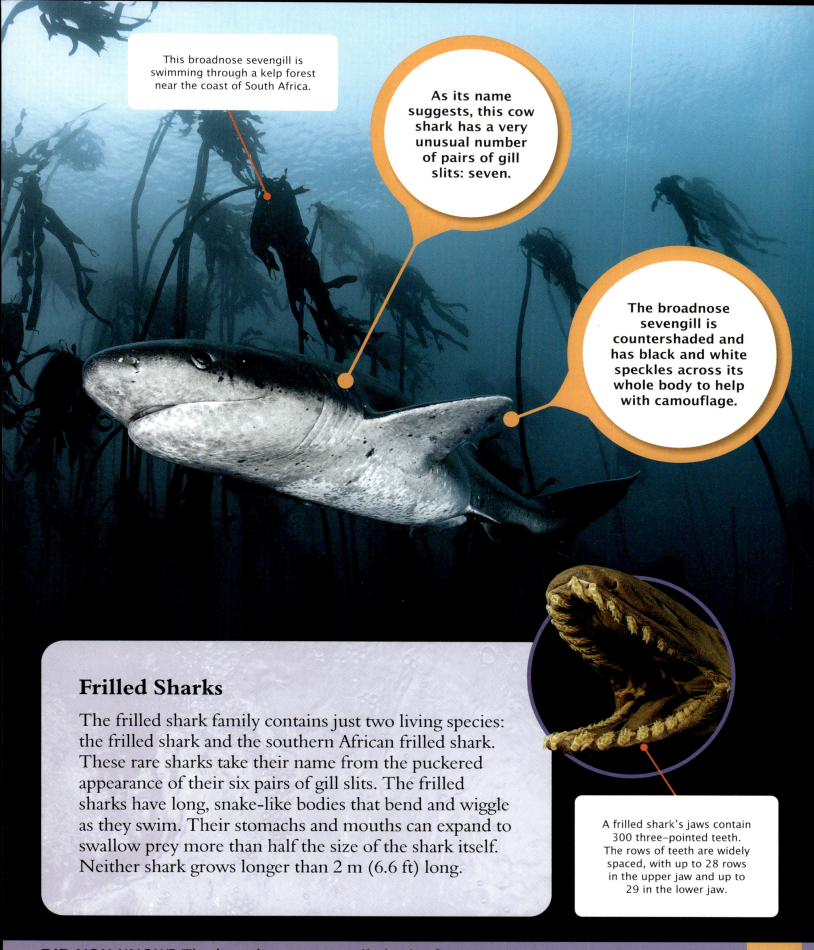

This broadnose sevengill is swimming through a kelp forest near the coast of South Africa.

As its name suggests, this cow shark has a very unusual number of pairs of gill slits: seven.

The broadnose sevengill is countershaded and has black and white speckles across its whole body to help with camouflage.

Frilled Sharks

The frilled shark family contains just two living species: the frilled shark and the southern African frilled shark. These rare sharks take their name from the puckered appearance of their six pairs of gill slits. The frilled sharks have long, snake-like bodies that bend and wiggle as they swim. Their stomachs and mouths can expand to swallow prey more than half the size of the shark itself. Neither shark grows longer than 2 m (6.6 ft) long.

A frilled shark's jaws contain 300 three-pointed teeth. The rows of teeth are widely spaced, with up to 28 rows in the upper jaw and up to 29 in the lower jaw.

DID YOU KNOW? The broadnose sevengill shark often scavenges, eating dead animals that are floating in the water or lying on the seafloor.

BULLHEAD SHARKS
Horn Shark

This shark is a member of the bullhead shark order. These small, nocturnal sharks are named for their bull-like appearance: a large head in comparison with their body, along with a ridge above each eye shaped rather like a bull's horn.

Sharp Spines

The bullhead sharks have a long spine at the front of each of their two tall dorsal fins. The spines are made of dentine and covered by enameloid, which are extremely strong, hard materials also found in human teeth. By curling and twisting their body, the bullhead sharks use their spines to defend themselves against predators. In addition, predators such as angelsharks have been seen spitting out horn sharks after finding their spines too sharp to swallow.

The horn shark has spines more than 5 cm (2 in) long.

The horn shark's supraorbital ridge is covered by extra-large, thick dermal denticles.

Brow Ridges

Like most bottom-dwellers, bullhead sharks have eyes positioned high on their head to give a better view over algae and rocks. Like many small animals, their eyes are also on their sides of their head so they can watch all around for predators. The thick, bony ridge above each eye, known as a supraorbital (meaning "above eye") ridge, shields the eyes from the glare of sunlight. It also makes the bright eyes harder to spot by predators swimming overhead.

DID YOU KNOW? Compared with its body size, the horn shark has the strongest bite of any shark—which it uses for crushing shells.

HORN SHARK

Heterodontus francisci

Bullhead shark

Length: 0.8 to 1.2 m (2.6 to 3.9 ft)
Range: Coasts of Mexico and the United States in the Pacific Ocean
Habitat: Rocky reefs and algae beds in tropical waters to 200 m (660 ft) deep
Diet: Oysters, sea urchins, shrimp, crabs, and small fish
Conservation: Unknown

During the day, this shark rests on thick mats of algae, where its golden-brown, spotted body is well camouflaged.

The horn shark relies less on electroreception to find prey, as it has only 148 ampullae of Lorenzini, compared with more than 2,000 in some sharks.

Bullhead sharks have a wide snout with large, trumpet-like nostrils, which help these bottom-dwellers to smell prey.

Japanese Bullhead Shark

The Japanese bullhead is a slow-moving, sluggish shark. It feeds on bottom-living, hard-shelled prey, which it grinds up with its strong back teeth before swallowing—but it usually brings up and spits out big bits of shell later.

Spiral Egg Cases

Like other bullhead sharks, the Japanese bullhead lays eggs. Bullhead shark egg cases are differently shaped from those of other sharks. Their egg cases are cone-shaped, with a large ridge twisting around the outside. Like the twisting groove on a screw, this shape anchors the eggs in crevices among rocks and coral, so they cannot be removed by predators.

It takes several hours for a female Japanese bullhead shark to lay each egg, due to the awkward, ridged shape of its case.

While it lies on the bottom, the Japanese bullhead shark sucks in water through its spiracle so its gills can continue to take oxygen.

JAPANESE BULLHEAD SHARK

Heterodontus japonicus

Bullhead shark

Length: 0.7 to 1.2 m (2.3 to 3.9 ft)
Range: Coasts of Japan, Korea, and China in the Pacific Ocean
Habitat: Coral reefs, rocky seafloors, and kelp forests in temperate waters to 37 m (121 ft) deep
Diet: Sea urchins, snails, shrimp, crabs, and small fish
Conservation: Least concern

The Japanese bullhead rests during the day, then hunts at night, often "walking" across the seafloor using its wide pectoral and pelvic fins.

Little Mouth

The bullhead sharks have little mouths that are positioned at the front of their snouts. Such mouths are suited to picking up or sucking up small, slow-moving prey. These sharks have small, cone-shaped front teeth that are used for grasping. Their back teeth are round, broad, and flat, making them ideal for crushing shells.

Like other bullhead sharks, the crested bullhead shark has a small mouth, which is joined to its nostrils by deep grooves.

This shark is camouflaged by dark bands that break up its outline, making it harder for predators to spot.

DID YOU KNOW? Female Japanese bullheads lay their eggs in the same patch as other females in their school, making them one of the few sharks to share a nest.

SAWSHARKS

Longnose Sawshark

Like other members of the sawshark order, the longnose sawshark has a saw-like snout known as a rostrum, which it uses to catch prey. Its rostrum is the longest among all the sawsharks, reaching a length of 40 cm (16 in).

Digging Rostrum

A longnose sawshark's rostrum is edged with sharp teeth, which alternate between long and short. Like the teeth inside the shark's mouth, these teeth are replaced when they fall out. The teeth help to stir up the sand as the sawshark uses its rostrum to dig in the seafloor for small, hiding prey. The sawshark also uses its rostrum to swipe at swimming fish by waving it quickly from side to side—stunning and slashing prey with its weight and teeth.

The longnose sawshark can live for up to 15 years.

A longnose sawshark's rostrum is dotted with tiny ampullae of Lorenzini (see page 60), which detect the electric fields created by moving prey.

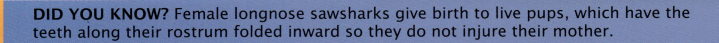

DID YOU KNOW? Female longnose sawsharks give birth to live pups, which have the teeth along their rostrum folded inward so they do not injure their mother.

Having a Rest

Schools of longnose sawsharks spend the daytime resting on the seafloor, where they are well camouflaged by their sandy, blotchy dermal denticles. When predators pass, a sawshark's flattened body lets it lie low. Sawshark predators include larger sharks, such as great whites, as well as human beings.

Longnose sawsharks can often be seen raised on their pectoral fins on the seafloor, giving them a wide view of the surrounding area.

At the middle of the rostrum is a pair of sensitive barbels, which the sawshark uses to feel, taste, and smell prey hiding in sand and gravel.

Unlike sawfish, which have gill slits on the underside of their head, sawsharks have gill slits on the sides of their head.

LONGNOSE SAWSHARK

Pristiophorus cirratus

Sawshark

Length: 1 to 1.3 m (3.3 to 4.3 ft)
Range: Coast of southern Australia in the Indian and Pacific Oceans
Habitat: Sandy or gravel seafloors in temperate waters to 310 m (1,017 ft) deep
Diet: Small fish, shrimp, crabs, and squid
Conservation: Least concern

151

ANGELSHARKS

Japanese Angelshark

The angelsharks take their name from their wide pectoral fins, which are said to look like angels' wings. Like its relatives, the Japanese angelshark is an ambush predator that lies in wait for prey, although it may swim in search of food at night.

The wide pectoral and pelvic fins are held horizontally as the shark swims, powered largely by its long, waving tail.

Hiding …

During the day, Japanese angelsharks bury themselves in the seafloor. They do this by slapping the ground with their body and pectoral and pelvic fins, sending up showers of sand and pebbles until they are hidden. Their speckled skin and flattened body shape also help to keep them camouflaged.

Only the Japanese angelshark's eyes are left uncovered, so it can watch for prey.

JAPANESE ANGELSHARK

Squatina japonica

Angelshark

Length: 1.5 to 2 m (4.9 to 6.6 ft)
Range: Coasts of Japan, Korea, and China in the Pacific Ocean
Habitat: Sandy seafloors in temperate waters to 300 m (980 ft) deep
Diet: Fish, shrimp, octopus, and squid
Conservation: Critically endangered

DID YOU KNOW? This angelshark is fished for its skin, known as shagreen, which is used to cover items such as photo frames and decorative boxes.

The Japanese angelshark's two small dorsal fins are positioned behind the pectoral fins.

Unusually for a shark, the lower lobe of the caudal fin is slightly longer than the upper lobe.

... And Attacking

When a Japanese angelshark senses approaching prey, it lunges upward from its hiding place and shoots out its jaws, which can swing both upward and outward. Like those of all sharks, its jaws are not fixed to its skull. The shark sucks prey into its mouth, pinning and ripping with its sharp, cone-shaped teeth.

This Japanese angelshark has flexed its neck and thrust out its jaws to catch a silver-stripe round herring.

Chapter 5: Other Cartilaginous Fish

Cartilaginous Evolution

> The bowmouth guitarfish is in the Rhinopristiformes order of rays, in the Elasmobranchii subclass of the Chondrichthyes class of fish.

Unlike other fish, sharks and their close relatives have skeletons made of light, bendy cartilage rather than bone. Known as cartilaginous fish, they make up a class of fish known as Chondrichthyes.

First Fish

Tiny, simple living things appeared in Earth's oceans around 3.5 billion years ago. Through slow changes, known as evolution, the first fishlike animals were swimming by 530 million years ago. Early fish had cartilage-like skeletons and no jaws, so they could not bite. Today's fish are in three groups known as classes: Agnatha, containing 120 species that still have a cartilaginous skeleton and no jaws; Chondrichthyes, containing around 1,050 species that evolved jaws but have a cartilaginous skeleton; and Osteichthyes, with 33,000 species of jawed fish that evolved bony skeletons.

Although it did not have a well-defined head, *Pikaia* was a fishlike animal that lived between 513 and 505 million years ago.

BOWMOUTH GUITARFISH
Rhina ancylostoma
Rhinopristiform ray

Length: 1.5 to 2.7 m (4.9 to 8.9 ft)
Range: Indian and Pacific Oceans
Habitat: Sandy and muddy seafloors in tropical waters to 90 m (300 ft) deep
Diet: Fish, crabs, shrimp, and clams
Conservation: Critically endangered

DID YOU KNOW? The bowmouth guitarfish is fished for its meat, fins, and thornlike dermal denticles, which are used to make bracelets.

Like most cartilaginous fish, it has skin covered in sharp scales known as dermal denticles, which contain similar materials to human teeth.

Two tall dorsal fins help with stability and making sudden turns.

Class of Chondrichthyes

Unlike most bony-skeletoned fish, Chondrichthyes do not have a gas-filled organ known as a swim bladder to help them float. All Chondrichthyes can sense the electric fields given off by prey using organs known as ampullae of Lorenzini. The Chondrichthyes are divided into two subclasses: Elasmobranchii, containing sharks and rays; and Holocephali, containing chimaeras. Like sharks, most rays have replaceable teeth, toothlike scales, and visible gill slits. Unlike sharks, most rays have a flattened body with gill slits on the underside. Chimaeras do not have replaceable teeth, toothlike scales, or visible gill slits.

Living 382 to 299 million years ago, *Stethacanthus* was an early member of the Chondrichthyes class. Its anvil-shaped first dorsal fin may have frightened away predators.

155

Guitarfish

Guitarfish are named for their flattened, guitar-shaped body. They are in the family of rays known as Rhinobatidae (meaning "nose ray"), due to having a longer snout than most rays. Around 36 guitarfish species live in tropical to warm temperate oceans close to coasts.

A Ray's Underside

Like most rays, guitarfish have their mouth on their underside, which is useful for sucking up small animals that live in or on the seafloor. Since guitarfish spend much of their time lying on the seafloor, they do not breathe by taking in water through their mouth but by sucking it through their spiracles, which are holes behind their eyes on the upper side of their body. The used water passes out of gill slits. Unlike sharks, which have their gill slits on the sides of their head, rays have gill slits under their pectoral fins.

Guitarfish and other rays have wide pectoral fins that are fused to their body.

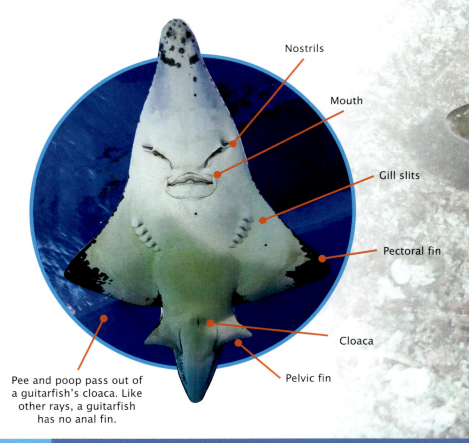

Pee and poop pass out of a guitarfish's cloaca. Like other rays, a guitarfish has no anal fin.

DID YOU KNOW? Guitarfish have been swimming in the oceans for at least the past 94 million years.

156

In low light, a banded guitarfish's pupils are large and round, but in bright light a tough, shiny tissue containing cartilage prevents too much light entering the eye.

Unusual Eyes

Guitarfish eyes have pupils (holes through which light passes into the eye) that narrow in bright light until they form a shape like a scribbled W. This shape is useful in shallow water, where it is often sunny above and dim below, as it evens out glare and shadow. Since guitarfish cannot close their eyelids, they pull their eyeballs 4 cm (1.6 in) back into their head to protect them when burrowing in sand or attacking prey.

Unlike most rays, guitarfish swim by moving their caudal (tail) fin from side to side, in the same manner as many sharks.

The Gorgona guitarfish's speckled, blotchy dermal denticles keep it camouflaged as it waits for bottom-living prey.

GORGONA GUITARFISH

Pseudobatos prahli

Rhinopristiform ray

Length: 70 to 90 cm (28 to 35 in)
Range: Coasts of Central and South America in the eastern Pacific Ocean
Habitat: Sandy and rocky seafloors in tropical waters to 70 m (230 ft) deep
Diet: Crabs, shrimp, worms, and clams
Conservation: Vulnerable

Sawfish

These rays have a saw-like snout, known as a rostrum. The rostrum is dotted with thousands of ampullae of Lorenzini, which are organs that sense the electric fields made by moving prey. When prey is detected, sawfish use their sharp-edged rostrum for swiping and pinning.

Sawfish vs Sawsharks

Sawfish are often confused with sawsharks, due to their similar-looking rostrums. However, sawfish are more closely related to other rays than to sawsharks. The similarity between sawfish and sawsharks is an example of convergent (meaning "coming closer together") evolution, which is when two different groups of animals evolve to have the same features because they are useful for the same purpose: in this case, finding and catching prey using their snout.

Up to 140 cm (55 in) long, the rostrum is made of cartilage covered in skin.

Unlike a sawshark, a sawfish (pictured) has gill slits on its underside. The teeth along a sawfish's rostrum are all the same length, while a sawshark's alternate between long and short. Sawfish do not have sensory barbels on their rostrum, but sawsharks do.

Along each side of its rostrum, the smalltooth sawfish has up to 32 "teeth," which are actually enlarged dermal denticles that are not replaced if they fall out.

DID YOU KNOW? Sawfish are among the world's most endangered fish, due to overfishing and damage to the shallow coastal habitats where females give birth.

SMALLTOOTH SAWFISH

Pristis pectinata

Rhinopristiform ray

Length: 5 to 5.5 m (16.4 to 18 ft)
Range: Atlantic Ocean
Habitat: Coastal seafloors in tropical and subtropical waters to 122 m (400 ft) deep
Diet: Fish, shrimp, and crabs
Conservation: Critically endangered

The smalltooth sawfish often rests on the seafloor, while the ampullae of Lorenzini along the top of its rostrum detect prey swimming overhead.

Sawfish Magic

For thousands of years, people living in coastal regions have told stories, created art, and performed dances about sawfish. Due to their strange rostrum, sawfish have been seen as magical, dangerous, and linked with the world of spirits and gods. In Africa's Gambia, sawfish rostrums were displayed in homes as symbols of fishermen's bravery. In Southeast Asia, they were hung over doorways to keep out ghosts. In Nigeria and the Bissagos Islands of Guinea-Bissau, dancers wore sawfish masks during ceremonies and celebrations.

This African sawfish mask was made from wood and shell in the early 20th century.

159

River Stingrays

Unlike most rays, the river stingrays usually live in freshwater. They are found in South American rivers, where they often lie on the bottom, partly buried in sand or mud. When prey nears, these fish raise their head by pressing down with their pectoral fins, then suck hard with their mouth.

Stinging Spine

A stingray has one or two sharp spines on its tail. The spines are covered in venom, a liquid that causes pain, swelling, and infection if it is injected into predators by a prick from the spine. Stingrays use their spines only to defend themselves, but sometimes human swimmers and waders are stung when they fail to spot stingrays buried on the river floor.

This stingray's stinger is covered in a sheath of skin and hooked dermal denticles that widen any wound made by the sting.

A stingray's stinger is usually covered by skin, which rips open when the stinger is used (pictured). The fish stings by waving its tail so the spine pierces its own skin covering and pricks the predator's skin.

POLKA DOT STINGRAY

Potamotrygon leopoldi

Myliobatiform ray

Length: 30 to 75 cm (12 to 30 in)
Range: Xingu and Fresco Rivers in Brazil, South America
Habitat: Sandy floors in tropical river water
Diet: Snails and crabs
Conservation: Not known

Waving Along

Unlike sharks, which usually swim by beating their caudal fin, stingrays swim by waving their wide, curving pectoral fins. Waves of movement travel along the pectoral fins from front to back. This swimming style does not create fast movement, but it also does not use a lot of energy.

Turns are made by waving one pectoral fin more than the other, but stingrays' wide, flattened bodies are not suited to sudden changes of direction.

When lying on the river floor, a stingray takes in water through its spiracles rather than its mouth.

The polka dot stingray's disk-shaped body is up to 40 cm (16 in) wide.

DID YOU KNOW? Stingrays shed and replace their venomous spine every 6 to 12 months, with the new spine often growing while the old one is still in place.

Mobula Rays

These rays are often called "flying rays" due to their habit of leaping out of the water, known as breaching. The mobula family includes the devil rays and manta rays, which are famed both for their great size and their great intelligence.

The devil rays are named for their cephalic fins, which look a little like devil's horns.

Clever Fish

With a brain weighing up to 200 g (7 oz), the giant oceanic manta ray has the heaviest brain compared to its body weight of any fish. These rays show their intelligence by playing with and forming friendships with others in their school. When manta rays meet an unknown manta, the white patches on their shoulders brighten. Yet when shown their reflection in a mirror, the white patches stay the same, as manta rays seem to recognize the reflection as themselves. This "mirror test" is not passed by most animals or even by very young humans.

Giant oceanic manta rays often go together to areas known as "cleaning stations," where fish, such as remoras, feed on their irritating parasites.

MUNK'S DEVIL RAY

Mobula munkiana
Myliobatiform ray

Length: 1 to 2.2 m (3.3 to 7.2 ft)
Range: Eastern Pacific Ocean
Habitat: Tropical waters to 15 m (49 ft) deep
Diet: Zooplankton, shrimp, and small fish
Conservation: Vulnerable

DID YOU KNOW? Up to 7 m (23 ft) across, the giant oceanic manta ray is one of the largest fish, with only a few species of sharks growing bigger.

Like other mobula rays, the Munk's devil ray jumps to show off to a mate, to communicate with its school, or to knock parasites off its body as it slaps back down.

Fine Fins

Mobula rays swim by moving their triangular pectoral fins up and down, like a bird flapping its wings. The pectoral fins have horn-shaped extensions, known as cephalic fins, on either side of the ray's mouth. When mobula rays are feeding, they stretch their cephalic fins forward to funnel water into their open mouth and through their gills. Mobula rays are filter feeders: They filter tiny animals, known as zooplankton, out of the water using sieve-like pads in their mouth. Water flows out through the gills, while food is caught on the pads.

Munk's devil rays have a long, stingless tail, which is not used for swimming or steering.

As a manta ray feeds, it flies through the water by flapping its pectoral fins, sending water into its open mouth.

Electric Rays

The electric rays make electricity, which they use to stun prey and defend themselves. Like other rays, electric rays have a flattened body and large pectoral fins. Yet, unlike other rays and sharks, these fish have soft skin with no covering of dermal denticles.

Making Electricity

An electric ray has two large electricity-making organs, on either side of its head. Each organ contains thousands of cells named electrocytes, which make electricity by stimulating electrically charged atoms. The electric charge travels into the surrounding water. The power of an electric ray's organs ranges from 8 to 220 volts. Household electricity has a force of around 230 volts in most of the world. The most powerful organs belong to the Atlantic torpedo, which emits enough electricity to stun large predators.

The outlines of the leopard torpedo's electricity-making organs can be seen on the underside of its body.

The panther torpedo ray's rounded pectoral fins, which are fused with its head and body, form an almost circular disk.

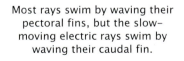

Most rays swim by waving their pectoral fins, but the slow-moving electric rays swim by waving their caudal fin.

PANTHER TORPEDO RAY

Torpedo panthera

Torpediniform ray

Length: 28 to 98 cm (11 to 39 in)
Range: Western Indian Ocean
Habitat: Coral reefs and muddy or sandy seafloors in tropical waters to 100 m (328 ft) deep
Diet: Small fish, shrimp, and crabs
Conservation: Not known

Pouncing on Prey

Electric rays spend much of their time resting on the seafloor, usually partly buried in sand. When small fish or other little animals pass by, electric rays pounce, wrapping their body around them while delivering a strong electric shock. The stunned prey is moved into the ray's mouth using rippling movements of its pectoral fins.

The marbled electric ray buries itself on the seafloor, leaving only its eyes and spiracles exposed.

The torpedo rays take their name from the Latin word *torpidus* ("paralysed"), due to making small pulses of electricity to warn away predators or large, stunning shocks.

DID YOU KNOW? Ancient Greek doctors used electric rays to deliver numbing shocks to patients just before operating on them.

Skates

Skates are a family of rays with a kite-shaped body and a stiff snout. Their long, slender tail contains an electricity-making organ. Unlike the electric rays, skates can make only a weak electric charge, which may be used for attracting the attention of a mate.

> Tall, thornlike dermal denticles surrounding the head give protection from predators.

Safe on the Seafloor

Skates are bottom-dwellers, spending most of their time lying on the seafloor, partly buried in sand or gravel, or gliding close to the bottom as they search for prey. Skates are well camouflaged from both prey and predators by having flattened bodies covered in sandy, speckled dermal denticles. In addition, many skates have eyespots (markings shaped like eyes) on the upper side of their pectoral fins, which frighten away predators.

The large eyespots of the Velez skate make predators think the skate is much larger than it is.

DID YOU KNOW? Little skates have been seen walking over the seafloor using first their left pelvic fin and then their right.

Old, empty skate egg cases are often found washed up on beaches.

Horned Egg Cases

Unlike their ray relatives, which give birth to live pups, skates lay eggs. These are protected by tough, leathery egg cases. Most skate species lay small cases, around 8 cm (3 in) long, containing one egg. Yet some skates lay larger cases holding up to seven eggs. Skate egg cases are more rectangular than those of egg-laying sharks. They have a curving horn at each corner, which catches on seaweed or rocks to stop them drifting into deep waters. The egg cases are waterproof at first, but soon after the growing babies have developed gills, holes open in the tips of the horns, letting seawater flow inside.

A little skate's 38 to 66 rows of small, round teeth are suited to crushing shelled prey.

The little skate's mouth is surrounded by ampullae of Lorenzini, which help it home in on small creatures hiding in the sand and gravel.

LITTLE SKATE

Leucoraja erinacea

Rajiform ray

Length: 41 to 54 cm (16 to 21 in)
Range: Northwestern Atlantic Ocean
Habitat: Sandy or gravel seafloors in temperate waters to 90 m (300 ft) deep
Diet: Crabs, shrimp, and worms
Conservation: Least concern

Chimaeras

These strange fish are usually found in deep, dark ocean water. In Greek myths, chimaeras were monsters with body parts of different animals, such as a lion's head and a serpent's tail. Real-life chimaeras have a large head, with a ducklike snout, and a long, slender tail.

> A female rabbit fish lives for up to 26 years and is able to lay eggs once she is 11 years old.

A Different Path

Chimaeras share the cartilaginous skeleton of sharks and rays, but around 400 million years ago, the ancestors of chimaeras started to evolve differently from their relatives. Unlike sharks and most rays, chimaeras have naked, rubbery skin without a covering of dermal denticles. They also do not have replaceable teeth, instead having three pairs of permanent tooth plates suited to grinding. Rather than five to seven pairs of visible gill slits, they have one pair of gill slits protected by covers, like the bony fish.

The spotted ratfish, like other chimaeras, has large eyes for seeing in dim water close to the ocean floor.

DID YOU KNOW? For attracting or holding females, male chimaeras have small spiky clubs that can be folded out from their forehead.

RABBIT FISH

Chimaera monstrosa

Holocephali

Length: 0.4 to 1.5 m (1.3 to 4.9 ft)
Range: Northeastern Atlantic Ocean
Habitat: Close to the seafloor in temperate waters to 1,400 m (4,590 ft) deep
Diet: Crabs, worms, octopus, and sea urchins
Conservation: Vulnerable

The venomous spine is raised to prick predators and lowered while swimming.

Chimaeras swim by flapping their winglike pectoral fins as they wiggle their long body.

Significant Spines

To protect them from predators, chimaeras have a sharp spine at the front of their first dorsal fin. It is covered in mild venom that causes pain when injected. Many fossils of ancient chimaera spines have been found, suggesting there were more chimaeras in the past than today, some of them living in shallow water. Today, there are only around 50 chimaera species.

The smallspine spookfish has a venomous spine up to 10 cm (4 in) long. Its snout is dotted with ampullae of Lorenzini that help it find prey.

Chapter 6: Bony Fish

Flatfish

> The wide-eyed flounder has both eyes on its left side. Like other flatfish, it can stick up its eyes to get a better view.

Like most fish, flatfish have skeletons made of bone. They live on the seafloor of all oceans, from the Arctic to the shores of Antarctica. With their flattened body, they are able to lie on their side as they wait—motionless—for passing prey.

Camouflage

Many flatfish are well camouflaged on the seafloor. Although their underside (which may be the left or right side) is pale, their upperside is usually dappled or spotted, to match the seabed. Some flatfish, such as flounder, can change their skin color, releasing pigments to make darker or lighter, smaller or bigger, spots.

This sole is burying itself in sand for extra camouflage. At night, it feeds on worms, mollusks, and small crustaceans.

Moving Eyes

When flatfish hatch from their eggs, they are symmetrical, with one eye on each side of their body. At this stage, they drift through the water rather than living on the bottom. As flatfish grow into adults, one of their eyes moves to the other side of the head. Then the flatfish sinks to the bottom, laying its eyeless side on the floor.

Depending on the species, flatfish have their left or right side uppermost. The European plaice has its right side uppermost.

DID YOU KNOW? Peacock flounders change color to suit their surroundings in 8 seconds, unless one of their eyes is covered by sand, which prevents them color matching.

TURBOT
Scophthalmus maximus

Length: 40 to 100 cm (16 to 39 in)

Range: European coasts of the northern Atlantic Ocean

Habitat: Sandy or rocky seabeds at depths of 20 to 70 m (65 to 230 ft)

Diet: Fish, crustaceans, and bivalves

Conservation: Population shrinking

Turbot

This flounder is waiting to ambush fish and shrimp.

The dorsal fin extends right round the head. Flatfish belong to the subclass of ray-finned fish, so their fins are supported by bony spines called rays.

171

Seahorses

These small fish are not covered in scales but in thick bony plates. This makes them unable to wiggle their bodies to swim, so they flutter their fins to move along slowly. In fact, seahorses are such bad swimmers that they usually remain still, using their curling tail to grip seaweed or coral.

Fathers Giving Birth

Seahorses have a unique method of giving birth. Before mating, a male and female seahorse court each other, dancing snout to snout and holding tails. When she is ready, the female seahorse puts 50 to 1,500 eggs into a pouch on the male's front. The male carries the eggs until they hatch, then releases the tiny young, called fry, into the water.

This male dwarf seahorse is releasing his fry into the water.

The seahorse sucks up microorganisms and tiny crustaceans through its toothless snout.

Bargibant's pygmy seahorse

BARGIBANT'S PYGMY SEAHORSE

Hippocampus bargibanti

Length: 1.3 to 2.6 cm (0.5 to 1 in)

Range: Tropical coasts of the eastern Indian and western Pacific Oceans

Habitat: Sea fan corals at depths of 10 to 40 m (33 to 130 ft)

Diet: Tiny crustaceans

Conservation: Small population, which may need future protection

DID YOU KNOW? The world's slowest-moving fish is the dwarf seahorse, which has a top speed of only 1.5 m (5 ft) per hour.

The Pacific seahorse is one of the largest fish in its family, reaching a top length of 30 cm (12 in).

Seadragons

The three species of seadragons belong to the same family as seahorses. They also have body plates and long snouts for sucking up food. Unlike seahorses, which are among the few fish to swim upright, seadragons swim horizontally and do not have a curling tail. Male seadragons also take care of their eggs, but they carry them on their tail rather than in a pouch.

Seadragons are known for their extraordinary camouflage. The leafy seadragon is covered in leaf-like fronds, which make it look like floating seaweed.

A seahorse's bony plates are arranged in rings down its body. This protection makes a seahorse tricky for predators to bite.

Boxfish and Relatives

> The horned boxfish, also called the longhorn cowfish, lives on coral reefs.

Boxfish, sunfish, porcupinefish, pufferfish, and triggerfish all belong to an order of bony fish called Tetraodontiformes (meaning "four teeth" in ancient Greek). Their unusual jaws form a beak shape, with tooth-like bones that are often used for crushing hard-shelled invertebrates.

Strange Bodies

For protection, most fish in this order are covered in bony plates, sharp spines, or tough skin. Their bodies are rigid, so they do not wriggle to swim. Instead, they move by waving their fins. These fish are also known for their strange body shapes, which may be nearly square (boxfish), round (porcupinefish), or flattened (sunfish and triggerfish).

A sunfish has perhaps the strangest-looking body of all fish. It ends behind the dorsal and anal fins, making the fish look as if it has lost its back half.

Puffing Up

Porcupinefish and pufferfish have a very effective defence when they are threatened by predators. They fill their stretchy stomachs with water, puffing the fish up until they are too big for most predators to swallow. In addition, they are covered by sharp spines. If this were not enough, pufferfish and some porcupinefish are also extremely poisonous.

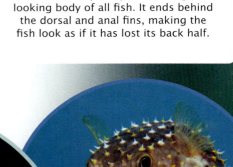

The yellowspotted burrfish is a poisonous species of porcupinefish that lives on coral reefs. It can inflate (right) to nearly twice its normal size (left).

174

CLOWN TRIGGERFISH
Balistoides conspicillum

Length: 40 to 50 cm (16 to 20 in)
Range: Tropical and subtropical coasts of the Indian and Pacific Oceans
Habitat: Coral reefs to depths of 75 m (250 ft)
Diet: Mollusks, crustaceans, and sea urchins
Conservation: Not known

Clown triggerfish

The tough horns make this fish harder to swallow. When threatened, the boxfish also releases poisonous mucus through its skin.

This boxfish eats algae, worms, crustaceans, and mollusks.

DID YOU KNOW? The ocean sunfish is the heaviest bony fish, weighing up to 2,300 kg (5,000 lb) and reaching 3.3 m (10.8 ft) long.

Surgeonfish and Relatives

Surgeonfish, tangs, and unicornfish usually live on coral reefs. On either side of their body, at the base of their tail, these fish have sharp spines like surgeon's knives. While some species have fixed spines, others have hinged spines that can be flicked out, with a twist of the tail, to wound predators.

Safety in Numbers

Fish in this family feed on algae that grows on coral reefs, grazing on it with their sharp teeth. Patches of algae are often guarded by aggressive damselfish. For this reason, surgeonfish and their relatives often feed in shoals, or groups, which offer defence against damselfish, as well as predators such as tuna and grouper.

These powder blue tangs are shoaling for safety. When the fish in a shoal are all swimming in the same direction, it is called schooling.

ORANGESPOT SURGEONFISH

Acanthurus olivaceus

Length: 20 to 35 cm (8 to 14 in)

Range: Tropical coasts of the eastern Indian and western Pacific Oceans

Habitat: Coral reefs to depths of 80 m (260 ft)

Diet: Algae and diatoms

Conservation: Not at risk

Orangespot surgeonfish

Growing up to 40 cm (16 in) long, the sohal surgeonfish lives on coral reefs in the Red Sea.

Surgeonfish play an important role on coral reefs, as they feed on algae, preventing overgrowth from damaging the coral.

This spine is normally folded against the body, pointing toward the head. When threatened, the fish flicks out the blade.

Unicornfish

As most unicornfish reach adulthood, they grow a bony, horn-like spike between their eyes. Males grow bigger horns than females. Scientists are not sure what use the horn has, since the fish do not use it for fighting, as is the case with horned mammals. It is likely the growth of the horn signals that a fish is big enough for mating.

The bluespine unicornfish has two fixed blue spines at either side of its tail.

DID YOU KNOW? The spines of the lined surgeonfish are venomous, causing painful wounds to humans and death to smaller predators.

177

Scorpionfish

Many of the world's most venomous species of fish are scorpionfish. These fish inject predators with venom by a prick from their sharp spines, which contain venom-making glands. Most species of scorpionfish live on or near the bottom of the world's warmer oceans.

Sucking Up

Scorpionfish capture prey using a method called suction feeding. Some scorpionfish lie in wait for prey while others hunt for it, but when prey comes close, they all behave the same way. In a fraction of a second, the scorpionfish opens its mouth and expands its cheeks. Water (and the prey in the water) rushes into the scorpionfish's mouth to fill the space.

The 13 long spines of the dorsal fin contain venom glands. There is also one venomous spine in each of the two pelvic fins and three in the anal fin, making 18 in total.

Reef Stonefish

The most venomous fish of all is the reef stonefish, which lives on coral reefs of the tropical Indian and Pacific Oceans. A prick from its spines can be deadly to humans, but luckily there is an antivenom available. What makes this fish dangerous to humans is its habit of sitting on the seafloor, looking just like a rock, as it waits for prey to ambush.

The well-camouflaged tasselled scorpionfish lies in wait for passing fish and crustaceans.

The reef stonefish is camouflaged to look like an algae-covered rock (right). Using its pectoral fins as spades, it can bury itself in sand to become even less visible (above right).

A member of the scorpionfish family, the common lionfish hunts at night for small fish and crustaceans.

SHORTFIN DWARF LIONFISH

Dendochirus brachypterus

Length: 12 to 17 cm (5 to 7 in)

Range: Tropical coasts of the Indian and western Pacific Oceans

Habitat: Coral reefs to depths of 80 m (260 ft)

Diet: Small crustaceans

Conservation: Not at risk

Shortfin dwarf lionfish

The fanlike pectoral fins are not venomous.

DID YOU KNOW? Lionfish are aposematic (from the ancient Greek for "away" and "sign"), which means their bold patterns warn predators that they are dangerous to eat.

179

Dragonets

These small fish live mainly in the tropical waters of the Indian and Pacific Oceans. Dragonets are usually brightly patterned, with large fins. These features are useful for attracting a mate. Dragonets stay close to sandy seafloors, where they bury themselves to escape predators.

Courting

Before mating, male and female dragonets court each other. During courtship, the two fish spread and display their fins. Then the pair swim upward side by side, rubbing against each other. Finally, near the water surface, the female releases her eggs and the male releases his sperm into the water. The fertilized eggs float away.

Like all dragonets, mandarin dragonets are sexually dimorphic, which means that males and females look different from each other. The male (on the left) is bigger, has longer fins, and is differently patterned.

Fighting

Male dragonets are very aggressive to one another. They most often fight over the right to mate with females, but sometimes they just fight to show their greater strength. During fights, the males chase, wrestle, and bite. Quite often, fights end in the death of the weaker male.

These two male painted dragonets are battling head to head. This species lives only around the coasts of Australia.

The picturesque dragonet's bright patterns help with camouflage in its coral reef habitat.

STARRY DRAGONET

Synchiropus stellatus

Length: 5 to 7.5 cm (2 to 3 in)

Range: Tropical coasts of the Indian and western Pacific Oceans

Habitat: Coral reefs at depths of 5 to 40 m (16 to 130 ft)

Diet: Small crustaceans, worms, and microorganisms

Conservation: Not known

Starry dragonet

Dragonets have large eyes, positioned on the top of their head. When the dragonet buries itself in sand for defence, its eyes stay uncovered to keep watch.

Dragonets do not have scales, so their skin is protected by a coating of thick, slimy mucus.

DID YOU KNOW? The mandarin dragonet got its name from its pattern, which is like the robes worn by "mandarin" officials who worked for the emperor of China.

Billfish

These large bony fish are fierce predators. They have long bills, or beaks, which are extensions of their upper jaw bones. The bills are used for slashing at prey—and occasionally for spearing it. Billfish include sailfish, marlins, and swordfish.

Fastest Fish

Billfish usually live in the open ocean, far from land. Their long, streamlined bodies and powerful muscles make them excellent swimmers. They travel vast distances in search of food and suitable water temperatures. When pursuing prey, billfish are the fastest fish in the ocean. Scientists do not agree which billfish is the fastest of all: some say it is the Indo-Pacific sailfish, while others name the black marlin, which has been recorded at 105 km/h (65 mph).

The Atlantic sailfish has a large, sail-like first dorsal fin, which it folds down while swimming. When attacking prey, it raises the sail to steady its side-to-side movement.

Found in the tropical and subtropical Indian and Pacific Oceans, the black marlin can grow to 4.65 m (15.3 ft) long.

Swordfish

The swordfish has the longest bill of all billfish, reaching 1.5 m (4.9 ft). While the bills of other billfish are rounder and more spearlike, the swordfish's is sword-shaped. It is flat, smooth, and sharp. Although some billfish have been known to spear prey, as well as predators such as great white sharks, swordfish use their bills only for slashing.

The swordfish hunts alone, chasing smaller fish such as mackerel and herring, as well as descending to find crustaceans and squid in the darker waters below.

DID YOU KNOW? The biggest billfish is the Indo-Pacific blue marlin, which reaches 5 m (16.4 ft) long and 625 kg (1,378 lb).

The sailfish slashes left to right with its jagged-edged bill, wounding fish to make them easier to catch.

This sailfish is attacking a shoal of sardines from behind, hoping to capture the slowest fish.

WHITE MARLIN
Kajikia albida

Length: 1.3 to 2.8 m (4.3 to 9.2 ft)
Range: Tropical and subtropical Atlantic Ocean
Habitat: Open ocean to depths of 100 m (330 ft)
Diet: Fish such as flying fish and tuna, as well as squid
Conservation: Population at risk from sport fishing and accidental capture in nets

White marlin

183

Anglerfish

On an anglerfish's head is a long growth, shaped like a fishing rod. At its end is a "lure" that looks like a little animal. The anglerfish wiggles the lure to attract prey, which it sucks into its large mouth.

The painted frogfish's lure looks like a fish.

Making Light

In the dark of the deep ocean, some anglerfish use light to attract prey. The lure at the end of their fishing rod has tiny light-making bacteria. These living things make the lure glow. The ability to make light is known as bioluminescence.

This whipnose anglerfish is attracting a fish with its glowing lure. The whipnose is named for its extremely long lure, which may be even longer than the fish's body. This anglerfish usually drifts motionless as it waits for passing prey, its lure swaying in the current.

Clinging On

In some anglerfish species, males are much smaller than females and cannot survive without them. Males must attach themselves to a female and be fed by her blood. This means that, when the female is ready to release eggs, the male is usefully close by.

A male headlight angler clings to a female with his teeth.

DID YOU KNOW? The male *Photocorynus spiniceps* anglerfish is probably the world's smallest fish, at just 6.2 mm (0.24 in) long.

PAINTED FROGFISH
Antennarius pictus

Length: 15 to 30 cm (6 to 12 in)
Range: Indian and Pacific Oceans
Habitat: Coral reefs in warm, shallow waters
Diet: Fish, shrimp, and crabs
Conservation: Not at risk

A painted frogfish with red shading

Over a few weeks, a frogfish can change its skin shade and pattern to match its surroundings.

Its mouth opens wide for prey as big as the frogfish.

185

Parrotfish

These fish are named for their unusual teeth, which form a hard beak, a little like a parrot's. Parrotfish use their beaks for scraping algae from coral and rocks. There are around 95 species of parrotfish, many of them living in the shallow coastal waters of the Indian and Pacific Oceans.

The rusty parrotfish lives on coral reefs in the Indian Ocean.

Changing Sex

In most species of parrotfish, all fish are born female. Later in their lives, usually when they have grown large, the females go through hormonal and body changes—and turn into males. This characteristic has probably evolved because small males are prevented from mating by bigger males, so it is more useful to be a female when small.

When a parrotfish changes from female to male, its scales usually change color, too. The female Mediterranean parrotfish is red and yellow, while males are silvery.

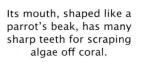

Its mouth, shaped like a parrot's beak, has many sharp teeth for scraping algae off coral.

DAISY PARROTFISH

Chlorurus sordidus

Length: 30 to 47 cm (12 to 19 in)
Range: Tropical Indian and Pacific Oceans
Habitat: Coral reefs and lagoons to 50 m (165 ft)
Diet: Algae
Conservation: Not at risk

Daisy parrotfish

186

The mucus of a parrotfish's protective balloon also contains chemicals that repel parasites.

Mucus Balloon

Before going to sleep, some parrotfish species blow mucus (a slimy, snotlike substance) out of their mouth, creating a mucus balloon. While wrapped in this balloon, the parrotfish cannot be smelt by predators. In addition, if a predator disturbs the balloon, the fish is woken before being hurt.

This parrotfish started life as a brown-scaled female, before changing both sex and appearance to become a bright-scaled male.

DID YOU KNOW? As it scrapes at rock and coral, a medium-sized parrotfish can create up to 90 kg (200 lb) of sand each year.

Chapter 7: Mammals

Baleen Whales

Along with dolphins and porpoises, whales belong to the group of marine mammals called cetaceans. Cetaceans power through the water with their tail, steering with their two flippers. They spend their whole life in the water, but surface to breathe air through the blowholes on top of their head. There are 15 species of baleen whales.

Baleen

Baleen whales are named for the plates of bristly baleen in their mouth. Baleen is made of keratin, the same tough material that makes human nails. When they feed, baleen whales take in a mouthful of water, either by lunge-feeding (taking a huge gulp) or skim-feeding (swimming with an open mouth). The water is then released through the baleen plates, which trap small prey inside the mouth.

This gray whale is showing its baleen plates. Gray whales are skim-feeders, scooping up sand, water, and tiny crustaceans as they swim over the seafloor. They live for up to 70 years.

Whale Song

All whales make sounds to communicate with each other. During mating season, male baleen whales are known for their "songs" to attract females. Songs are made up of moans, chirps, and roars. Humpback whales have the most complex songs, lasting 10 to 20 minutes, which are repeated for hours. During each mating season, all humpback males in one region sing the same song, which changes from one season to the next. Sometimes, males in one region copy songs from other regions.

Humpback whales often move in small groups called pods, containing mothers and their calves, but they gather in larger groups during mating season.

SOUTHERN RIGHT WHALE

Eubalaena australis

Length: 11 to 18 m (36 to 59 ft)
Range: Southern Ocean in southern summer; southern Atlantic, Indian, and Pacific Oceans in winter
Habitat: Open ocean in summer; coastlines in winter
Diet: Zooplankton and krill
Conservation: Population stable after huge losses due to hunting in previous centuries

Southern right whale

Barnacles often attach themselves to a humpback whale's skin.

The humpback whale, which reaches 16 m (52 ft) long, often leaps partway out of the water, called breaching.

The flippers have knobbles called tubercles. These are enlarged hair follicles, or roots from which hairs grow.

DID YOU KNOW? The largest animal that ever lived, the blue whale can hold 90,000 l (19,800 gallons) in its mouth, but cannot swallow anything bigger than a beach ball.

Toothed Whales

Sperm whales, beaked whales, and white whales all have teeth for catching prey, rather than baleen plates. While baleen whales have two blowholes, toothed whales have just one. Scientists also put dolphins and porpoises in the toothed whale group, but those cetaceans are usually smaller.

Echolocation

Sound travels fast and far underwater, unlike light, which does not reach far below the surface. With a method called echolocation, toothed whales use sound to navigate and find prey. They make clicking noises, which travel outward from the whale. The clicks bounce off objects and return. The speed and quality of the returning echoes allow toothed whales to build up a "picture" of their surroundings.

Like the other 22 species of beaked whales, Cuvier's beaked whale uses echolocation to dive deep for squid and fish. Its long jaw bones make a "beak," while the single blowhole is on top of its head.

White Whales

The beluga whale and narwhal (see pages 42–43) make up the family of white whales, which are found in and around the Arctic Ocean. Both these whales are quite small, reaching around 5 m (16 ft) long. They have bulbous heads, creating a "melon" on their forehead. Unlike most whales, they do not have a dorsal fin to help with steering.

The beluga whale dives in search of fish. Since its teeth are small and quite blunt, it has to swallow prey whole.

The sperm whale's squarish head often has scars from teeth scrapes made during battles with other whales.

As in all cetaceans, the tail, called the fluke, is horizontally flattened so it can beat up and down.

The sperm whale dives as deep as 2,250 m (7,380 ft) in search of giant squid.

SPERM WHALE
Physeter macrocephalus

Length: 11 to 20.5 m (36 to 67 ft)
Range: All oceans except Arctic and Southern Oceans where covered by ice
Habitat: Usually deep oceans away from coasts
Diet: Squid, sharks, rays, and other large fish
Conservation: Threatened by tangling in nets, collisions with boats, global warming, pollution, and ocean noise

Sperm whale breaching

DID YOU KNOW? A Cuvier's beaked whale holds the record for the longest underwater dive by a mammal: 137 minutes.

Dolphins

Dolphins are small toothed whales, with a streamlined body for fast swimming and cone-shaped teeth for grasping prey. Dolphins make a wide range of sounds to communicate with each other, from clicks to whistles. Around 30 species of dolphins live in the oceans, with another 4 species living in rivers.

Living in a Pod

Dolphins are very sociable, living in pods that differ in size from species to species. A small pod may contain just a mother and her calves. Sometimes, family groups join together to number over a hundred dolphins—or even thousands where there is plenty of prey. Dolphins show strong bonds between friends and relatives. They often help weaker members of their pod, staying beside injured friends or helping them to the surface to breathe.

Up to 8 m (26 ft) long, orcas are the largest dolphins, but are sometimes called killer whales. Pods are led by the oldest female and contain her children and their children.

Acrobatics

Dolphins often leap above the water surface. Sometimes this is the quickest way of travelling, as it is easier to move through air than water. At other times, dolphins leap to see what is going on, to show off to each other, to shake parasites off their skin—or just to play. Dolphins sometimes play in other ways, by chasing each other or by tossing around objects.

Spinner dolphins are named for their habit of spinning around as they leap through the air.

Common bottlenose dolphins are 2 to 4 m (6.6 to 13 ft) long and live for 40 to 50 years.

This dolphin gets its name from its beak, which looks a little like the neck of a bottle.

Common bottlenose dolphins live in pods of around 15, often working together to capture shoals of fish.

STRIPED DOLPHIN
Stenella coeruleoalba

Length: 2 to 2.4 m (6.6 to 7.9 ft)
Range: Temperate to tropical Atlantic, Indian, and Pacific Oceans
Habitat: Usually deep oceans away from coasts
Diet: Fish, squid, octopus, krill, and other crustaceans
Conservation: Population shrinking due to tangling in nets, collisions with boats, and pollution

Striped dolphins

DID YOU KNOW? The smallest dolphin is the critically endangered Maui's dolphin, which lives off the coast of New Zealand and reaches 1.7 m (5.6 ft) long.

193

Porpoises

Porpoises are closely related to dolphins, but they do not have beaks and have spade-shaped rather than cone-shaped teeth. There are seven species of porpoises, including the tiniest cetacean of all, the vaquita, which is just 1.4 m (4.6 ft) long.

Life at Sea

Female porpoises are pregnant for a full year before giving birth to just one calf in the water. Mothers produce milk, which is thick like toothpaste, so it can be squirted into the calf's mouth. The milk is high in fat, which helps the calf develop its thick layer of body fat, called blubber. As in all cetaceans, blubber keeps a porpoise warm, even in deep waters and polar regions.

Porpoises are preyed on by sharks and orcas. This orca is hurling a harbor porpoise through the air to weaken it for capture.

Most Endangered

The finless, narrow-ridged finless, and vaquita porpoises are all at risk of extinction. The vaquita is the most endangered cetacean of all, with only around 10 left in 2019. The vaquita lives in the northern Gulf of California, off the coast of Mexico. Major threats to the vaquita, and all other porpoises, include accidental capture in fishing nets and water pollution.

Since the finless porpoise lives in coastal waters, it is particularly at risk from human behavior.

Conservationists are working hard to save the last vaquitas. Even photos of this critically endangered cetacean are extremely rare.

DID YOU KNOW? Porpoises sleep with one eye and half their brain at a time, while the other side controls the blowhole and stays partly alert—then the porpoise swaps sides.

DALL'S PORPOISE

Phocoenoides dalli

Length: 1.8 to 2.3 m (5.9 to 7.5 ft)
Range: Temperate and subarctic northern Pacific Ocean
Habitat: Usually deep oceans away from coasts
Diet: Fish, squid, and crustaceans
Conservation: Population at risk in some areas from hunting

Dall's porpoise

Found along coasts in the northern hemisphere, the harbor porpoise has a small, rounded head with no beak.

Porpoises have large pupils, allowing plenty of light to enter the eye and giving good vision while diving deep for fish and squid.

The harbor porpoise's dorsal fin is almost triangular, helping the cetacean to steer.

Sea Cows

The sea cows, also called sirenians, are an order of mammals that live in warm and shallow water, ranging from coastal seas to swamps and rivers. They are mostly plant-eaters, using their strong lips to rip off leaves and stems. They have heavy bones and rounded bodies, making them slow swimmers.

The Dugong

The dugong, which reaches 3 m (10 ft) long and lives for up to 70 years, is one of the four species of sea cows. It lives in warm coastal waters of the Indian and Pacific Oceans. Like all sea cows, it has no dorsal fin or back limbs, but has flipper-like front limbs. Unlike its relatives, the manatees, its snout is downturned, which makes it easier to feed on bottom-growing seagrass. It has peglike teeth for grinding plants.

Manatees

There are three species of manatees. The West Indian and African manatees live both in coastal waters and nearby rivers and wetlands. The Amazonian manatee lives only in the Amazon River, in South America. Manatees usually swim alone, apart from mothers and their calves, which stay together for up to 18 months. Adults also form groups in the mating season.

The West Indian manatee lives on the warm eastern coast of the Americas, from the United States to Brazil, often swimming inland up rivers.

The dugong's two nostrils are closed by valves when it is underwater. It can last up to six minutes before going to the water surface to breathe.

This West Indian manatee calf is drinking milk from its mother. Her teats are just behind her flippers. Mothers and calves squeak to communicate with each other.

Like all mammals, the manatee has body hair. The manatee's hairs are extremely sensitive, allowing it to feel slight movements in the murky water.

The manatee's tail is flattened and paddle-like.

AFRICAN MANATEE
Trichechus senegalensis

Length: 3 to 4.5 m (9.8 to 14.8 ft)
Range: Tropical coasts of western Africa
Habitat: Shallow coastal ocean, rivers, and lakes
Diet: Mostly plants, including mangrove leaves and seagrass, as well as bivalves
Conservation: Population shrinking due to hunting and habitat loss

African manatee

DID YOU KNOW? The closest living relatives of sea cows are elephants, which are also plant-eating mammals with thick skin.

Polar Bear

The polar bear lives on and around the Arctic Ocean, where it hunts for its favourite food: seals. These bears are born on land, but spend most of their life on the ice that covers the ocean surface, sometimes diving into the cold water. They have thick body fat and fur to keep them warm.

Born in a Den

During the autumn when a female polar bear is pregnant, she digs a den in the snow, then climbs inside to rest. Snow soon covers the entrance, making it warm inside. Usually, the mother gives birth to two cubs, which start out completely blind. Although the mother has not eaten since entering her den, she feeds the cubs on her milk. In the spring, the family finally leaves the den and heads for the sea ice, where the mother hunts for prey for them all.

Cubs stay with their mother until they are about two and a half years old.

Hunting Seals

Polar bears usually catch seals when they come to holes in the ice to breathe. Bears use their powerful sense of smell to find a seal breathing hole, then crouch to wait. When a seal pops up, the bear drags it out with a clawed paw. Sometimes, polar bears creep close to seals that are resting on the ice, rushing forward in a final deadly attack.

Polar bears eat as many seals as possible from winter to summer, storing up energy for the late summer and autumn, when the sea ice melts and hunting is difficult.

DID YOU KNOW? The longest known underwater dive by a polar bear lasted 3 minutes and 10 seconds.

The bear can smell a seal at a distance of 1.6 km (1 mile).

The paws are large to help with swimming and to spread the bear's weight so it does not sink into snow or crash through thin sea ice.

A polar bear's coat appears white, but its hairs are actually colorless and see-through.

POLAR BEAR

Ursus maritimus

Length: 1.8 to 3 m (5.9 to 9.8 ft)

Range: The coastal Arctic Ocean and surrounding land

Habitat: Sea ice, ocean, and land when sea ice melts in late summer to autumn

Diet: Ringed, bearded, and other seals, plus bird eggs and dead walruses and whales

Conservation: Population at risk from global warming

Polar bear

Otters

There are 13 species of otters, which are meat-eating mammals that spend part or most of their lives in either saltwater or freshwater. Two species, the sea and marine otters, live only in saltwater, while the Eurasian otter moves between coastal oceans and rivers. All the other otters live around freshwater.

Sea Otter

Unlike other marine mammals, otters do not have blubber, so their slim bodies are covered in thick fur to keep them warm. The sea otter lives in coastal waters of the northern and eastern Pacific Ocean. Its back paws are wide and webbed for paddling, while the smaller front paws have sharp claws for catching prey. The sea otter dives to the seafloor in search of sea urchins, molluscs, crustaceans, and fish. This clever otter is known for using rocks to break open tough shells.

Sea otters sleep and rest together in large single-sex groups called rafts, sometimes holding each other's paws.

This sea otter is cracking open a clam on the side of a boat.

Eurasian otter

EURASIAN OTTER
Lutra lutra

Length: 0.9 to 1.4 m (3 to 4.6 ft)
Range: Rivers and coasts of Europe, North Africa, and Asia
Habitat: Rivers, lakes, and coastal oceans with freshwater nearby for washing off salt
Diet: Fish, crustaceans, insects, and birds
Conservation: Population shrinking in some regions due to habitat loss and pollution

To stop themselves from drifting out to sea while sleeping, the otters wrap themselves in kelp.

Sea otters float easily on their back, helped by air trapped in their fur.

Marine Otter

Unlike the sea otter, which spends nearly all its life in the ocean, the marine otter spends a lot of time on rocky beaches. It is found along the western coast of South America, where it hunts for crabs, molluscs, shrimps, and fish. Like the sea otter, the marine otter is endangered by oil spills and other pollution. In the past, it was hunted for its fur.

The marine otter's muscular tail helps with steering through the water.

DID YOU KNOW? The sea otter has the thickest fur of any animal, with up to 150,000 hairs per square cm (around 1 million per square inch).

Walrus

Although it is closely related to seals, the walrus is the only species in its family. The walrus has four flippers, long tusks, and whiskers. Its thick blubber makes it extremely heavy, sometimes weighing as much as 2,000 kg (4,400 lb), and keeps it warm in the freezing temperatures of the far north.

Whiskers

Walruses have mats of bristly whiskers, called vibrissae, on their snout. These hairs are linked to nerves, making them extremely sensitive. Walruses use their whiskers for feeling movement in the water and for finding prey on the muddy, dark seabed.

This walrus calf (left) and its mother (right) have 400 to 700 whiskers. The calf will stay with its mother for up to five years.

Tusks

Both male and female walruses have tusks, but a male's tusks are slightly longer, reaching up to 1 m (3.3 ft). Tusks are the walrus's canine teeth, which are the pointed, fanglike teeth in all mammals. Tusks are used for making breathing holes in the sea ice from the water below, and for help with climbing out onto slippery ice. Male walruses also use their tusks for fighting, to keep other males away from their mates.

Outside the mating season, hundreds of walruses crowd together in single-sex groups on beaches.

During mating season, male walruses often fight in the water. The largest males with the biggest tusks usually win.

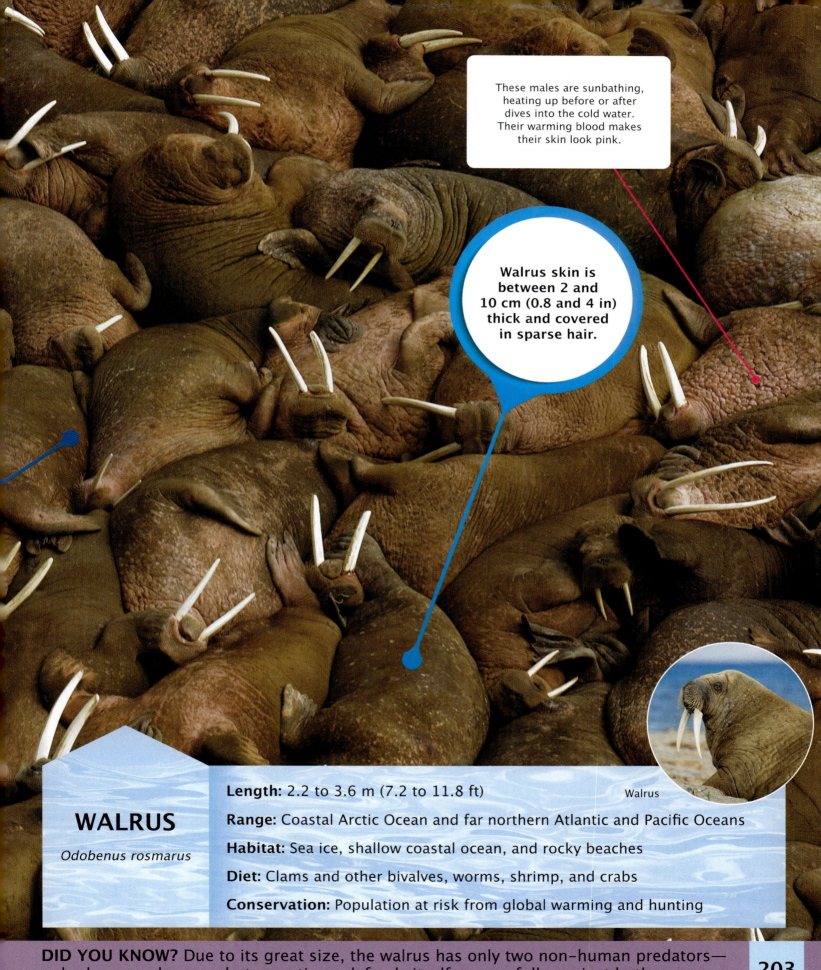

These males are sunbathing, heating up before or after dives into the cold water. Their warming blood makes their skin look pink.

Walrus skin is between 2 and 10 cm (0.8 and 4 in) thick and covered in sparse hair.

Walrus

WALRUS
Odobenus rosmarus

Length: 2.2 to 3.6 m (7.2 to 11.8 ft)
Range: Coastal Arctic Ocean and far northern Atlantic and Pacific Oceans
Habitat: Sea ice, shallow coastal ocean, and rocky beaches
Diet: Clams and other bivalves, worms, shrimp, and crabs
Conservation: Population at risk from global warming and hunting

DID YOU KNOW? Due to its great size, the walrus has only two non-human predators—polar bears and orcas—but sometimes defends itself successfully against both.

Seals

There are 18 species of true seals. They have a streamlined body suited to swimming and deep diving, with two large back flippers for paddling and two smaller, clawed front flippers for steering. Since their back flippers cannot be pulled under the body for walking, true seals have to wriggle along on land.

Fast Parenting

True seals are so well suited to life in the ocean that they rarely go ashore. However, they do come to land, or onto sea ice, to give birth. A mother gives birth to only one pup, which she feeds on extremely high-fat milk for just a few days or weeks, depending on the species. Then the mother must return to the sea to hunt so she can survive. The pup lives off the fat it has built up until it has learned to hunt for itself.

Living for up to 35 years, the harbor seal is found in coastal waters of the northern Atlantic and Pacific Oceans.

A young Weddell seal yelps to tell its mother it is hungry for milk.

Elephant Seals

The largest seal is the southern elephant seal, with males reaching 6 m (19.7 ft) long. Elephant seals are named for the male's large snout, which looks a little like an elephant's trunk. The hollow, muscly snout acts a bit like a horn, making the male's roars even louder. Elephant seals are able to hold their breath for more than 100 minutes, longer than any mammal that is not a cetacean.

A seal's eyes can see well underwater and in air. When diving, a nictitating membrane, or see-through third eyelid, covers the eyeball for protection.

The male elephant seal roars to warn away other males, who might try to compete for females.

Like other true seals, which are also known as earless seals, the harbor seal has no ear flaps around the openings to its ears.

ATLANTIC SEAL
Halichoerus grypus

Length: 1.6 to 3.3 m (5.2 to 10.8 ft)
Range: Coastal northern Atlantic Ocean
Habitat: Coastal ocean, rocks, islands, and beaches
Diet: Fish, octopus, and lobsters
Conservation: Population growing since bans on hunting

Atlantic seal

DID YOU KNOW? The Weddell seal lives farther south than any other mammal, since it lives on the sea ice surrounding Antarctica.

Eared Seals

Sea lions and fur seals are known as eared seals, because unlike true seals, the opening to their ear is covered by an ear flap. There are six species of sea lions and nine species of fur seals, which are found in all the world's oceans, apart from the Arctic and northern Atlantic Oceans.

Walking on All Fours

Unlike true seals, which have small front paws, eared seals have large front flippers. Their back flippers can also be turned forward, allowing eared seals to walk on all fours. This makes them much more agile when on land, where they spend more of their time than true seals. Large and noisy groups of sea lions or fur seals, called rookeries, can be seen on beaches. Female eared seals spend longer caring for their pups than true seals: up to a year. When mothers go hunting, pups often gather together to play.

These friendly female California sea lions have gathered underwater, close to their rookery.

The endangered Australian sea lion lives on the beaches and in the coastal waters of southwestern Australia.

NORTHERN FUR SEAL

Callorhinus ursinus

Length: 1.5 to 2.1 m (4.9 to 6.9 ft)
Range: Coastal northern Pacific Ocean
Habitat: Ocean and beaches
Diet: Fish and squid
Conservation: Population at risk from global warming, pollution, and tangling in nets

Northern fur seal rookery

DID YOU KNOW? Eared seals are known for their loud barking and honking to each other, but also make trumpet sounds when a predator has been spotted.

Female California sea lions are around 1.8 m (5.9 ft) long, while males average 2.4 m (7.9 ft) long.

Hair or Fur

Sea lions have short, rough hair, but fur seals have soft fur. Fur combines coarse "guard" hairs with thicker, softer underfur. During the eighteenth and nineteenth centuries, fur seals were widely hunted for their fur. Some species, including the Cape, northern, and Guadalupe fur seals, were hunted almost to extinction. Since hunting has been banned or limited by many countries, most species have slowly recovered.

The ear flaps, which direct sounds into the ear, allow the sea lion to hear well both above and below water.

When it is wet, the South American fur seal looks almost black, but its fur dries to gray or light brown.

207

Chapter 8: Reptiles

Sea Turtles

From smallest to largest, the seven species of sea turtles are the Kemp's ridley, olive ridley, hawksbill, flatback, green, loggerhead, and leatherback. A sea turtle's large but streamlined body is protected by a shell divided into two parts: covering the back is the carapace, while covering the underside is the plastron.

Nesting on a Beach

At the start of mating season, sea turtles swim from their feeding areas to their coastal mating areas, which may be thousands of miles away. When a female is ready to lay her eggs, she climbs onto the beach, usually at night, and digs a hole in the sand using her back flippers. She lays a clutch of soft-shelled eggs, covers them with smoothed sand to disguise the spot, then returns to the sea. After 50 to 60 days, female babies hatch from eggs that were kept warmer, while males hatch from cooler eggs.

Female loggerhead turtles always nest on the beach where they were born. They lay around 100 eggs in each nest, making about four nests per season. Just a handful of babies will survive to adulthood.

This olive ridley turtle is swimming through plastic rubbish, which it might mistake for food, clogging its stomach.

At Risk

Sea turtles are among the world's most threatened animals. The Kemp's ridley and hawksbill turtles are "critically endangered," while the green turtle is "endangered." The other species, apart from the flatback, are "vulnerable," which means they will become endangered if care is not taken. Threats faced by sea turtles include damage to their nesting beaches, water pollution, tangling in fishing nets, and rising sea temperatures.

FLATBACK TURTLE
Natator depressus

Length: 76 to 100 cm (30 to 39 in)
Range: Coastal waters of Australia and New Guinea, in the Indian and Pacific Oceans
Habitat: Tropical and subtropical waters with soft beds, at depths up to 60 m (200 ft)
Diet: Soft coral, shrimp, jellyfish, and sea cucumbers
Conservation: At risk from habitat damage and pollution

A flatback turtle hatchling

The hawksbill's mouth is sharp and hooked, like a beak, which makes it ideal for eating tough sea sponges, algae, and jellyfish.

Growing to around 114 cm (45 in) long, the hawksbill lives mainly on tropical coral reefs in the Atlantic, Indian, and Pacific Oceans.

The carapace is made up of 13 overlapping bony plates called scutes.

DID YOU KNOW? The longest-lived sea turtle is the green turtle, which can survive for more than 80 years in the wild.

209

Sea Crocodiles

Two species of crocodiles swim regularly in the oceans. Like most reptiles, the saltwater and American crocodiles are cold-blooded, which means their body becomes hotter or colder depending on the water and air temperature. These reptiles warm up after swimming by going ashore to bask in the sun.

Slightly larger than the American, the saltwater crocodile grows up to 6.3 m (20.7 ft) long.

The Saltwater Crocodile

The saltwater crocodile lives along the coasts of northern Australia and southern Asia. The largest living reptile, with jaws up to 98 cm (39 in) long, this crocodile is an apex predator. Its aggression makes it a threat not only to its common prey—which ranges from sharks to birds and crabs—but also to humans. The crocodile lies in wait, then swims at prey at up to 29 km/h (18 mph). It either drowns its victim, by pulling it underwater, or swallows it whole.

The saltwater crocodile has one of the strongest bites of any animal, due to its immensely strong, large jaw muscles.

AMERICAN CROCODILE

Crocodylus acutus

Length: 2.5 to 6 m (8.2 to 19.7 ft)
Range: Coasts of the Americas, from Florida, USA, to Peru, in the Atlantic and Pacific Oceans
Habitat: Coastal ocean, rivers, lakes, and swamps
Diet: Fish, frogs, turtles, birds, and small mammals
Conservation: Threatened by habitat loss

American crocodile

The American Crocodile

Like other crocodiles, the American crocodile has a streamlined body. It swims by beating its long, muscly tail, while steering with its webbed feet. The American crocodile's snout is long, narrow, and capable of opening wide to take prey as large as sea turtles. It has around 68 sharp teeth, set in jaws that are closed by strong muscles, giving it a deadly bite. The female lays 30 to 70 eggs in a mound of sand, mud, and leaves that she makes at the water's edge.

The American crocodile weighs up to 900 kg (2,000 lb).

Its skin is protected and waterproofed by tough bony plates called scutes.

The saltwater crocodile often hunts at night. Its vertical pupils can contract to a narrow slit so it is not dazzled in daylight.

DID YOU KNOW? Saltwater crocodiles have 66 teeth, with the longest ones (the fourth teeth from the front on the lower jaw) up to 9 cm (3.5 in) long.

Marine Iguana

The marine iguana is the only species of lizard that swims in the oceans. It lives only on the shores of the Galápagos Islands, in the Pacific Ocean, where it feeds on the algae that grow in shallow water. The iguana swims by waving its flattened tail from side to side.

Algae Eater

Seven or eight slightly different-looking subspecies of marine iguana have evolved on the different islands of the Galápagos archipelago. All of the subspecies eat algae. Females and smaller males eat algae exposed on the beach at low tide, or in shallow water. Large males, which reach 140 cm (55 in) long, can dive as deep as 30 m (98 ft) and spend up to 1 hour underwater while feeding. The marine iguana has heavier bones than a land iguana, which helps it dive to the bottom, where it pulls itself across rocks with its long claws.

The marine iguana's snout is short, with sharp three-pointed teeth, for scraping algae off rocks.

This marine iguana is grazing on algae on seabed rocks.

MARINE IGUANA
Amblyrhynchus cristatus

Length: 0.3 to 1.4 m (1 to 4.6 ft)
Range: Coasts of the Galápagos Islands in the Pacific Ocean
Habitat: Rocky shores
Diet: Algae, poop, and small invertebrates
Conservation: Threatened by invasive species

A male marine iguana turns pink in the mating season.

The iguana has a row of spines along its back.

Staying Warm

The sea surrounding the Galápagos Islands is cool, around 11 to 23 °C (52 to 73 °F), so the marine iguana warms up in the sunshine between swims. Its dark skin soaks up more sunlight than it reflects, which helps this reptile keep up its body temperature. At night, a colony of marine iguanas—which numbers between 20 and 500 or even 1,000—huddles together for warmth. Some iguanas also shelter among rocks or plants.

Colonies usually live on rocky shores, but are occasionally found on sandy beaches.

Like other lizards, as well as snakes, the marine iguana has skin covered in small, horny scales.

DID YOU KNOW? Young marine iguanas eat the poop of the adults in their colony, which gives them useful bacteria that will help with digesting algae.

213

Chapter 9: Birds
Plovers and Relatives

Plovers and their relatives are called waders or shorebirds. They often live on beaches and mudflats, where they search for invertebrates in the sand or mud. They are small to medium birds, with long legs for wading through the shallows. Many of them also have long beaks for probing.

> The wrybill is a species of plover that lives along the coasts of New Zealand, flying inland to nest beside rivers in spring.

Oystercatchers

Oystercatchers have large orange or red beaks that they use for opening the shells of mollusks such as oysters, mussels, and limpets. These birds usually attack their prey when the tide is going out, before the invertebrates have fully closed their shells after feeding. Oystercatchers also dig in soft sand and mud to find worms.

The Magellanic oystercatcher has yellow eyes, surrounded by a ring of yellow skin.

Black-necked stilt

BLACK-NECKED STILT
Himantopus mexicanus

Length: 34 to 36 cm (13 to 14 in)
Range: The Americas, from the United States to Argentina
Habitat: Coasts and wetlands
Diet: Small invertebrates, fish, and tadpoles
Conservation: Population shrinking in some regions due to habitat loss

DID YOU KNOW? Plovers get their name from the Latin word "*pluvia*," meaning rain, because people used to think they formed flocks when it was about to rain.

The wrybill's beak bends to the right, making it the only bird in the world with a beak that kinks to one side. The bend helps with reaching invertebrates hiding beneath rocks.

Avocets and Stilts

These waders have long, thin legs and beaks, as well as striking plumage, usually featuring black and white patches. Avocets feed by sweeping their upturned beak from side to side through shallow water or across the surface of mud, as they feel and look for shrimp, insects, and worms. Stilts usually hunt by sight alone, using their straight beak to jab into the water to seize small invertebrates and fish.

Gray and white plumage offers camouflage on stony or sandy shores and riverbeds.

These male and female American avocets are courting each other, bowing and swaying from side to side. Soon the pair will build a saucer-shaped nest of twigs close to the water.

215

Flamingos

The six species of flamingos live in tropical regions and the warm regions that border them, called subtropical areas, in the Americas, Africa, Asia, and Europe. Flamingos are waders, feeding in shallow seawater along coasts or in salty inland lakes.

Colony Life

Flamingos live in colonies of up to 100,000 birds. Living together means that birds can keep themselves and their nests safer. In the mating season, males and females break off into smaller groups that dance to each other, stretching their necks and flicking their heads from side to side. When the birds have formed pairs, they build a mound of mud on which to lay their single egg.

A group of flamingos performs a mating display.

Strange Standing ... and Walking

Flamingos often stand on one leg for long periods. Scientists think the birds take this pose because it uses less energy for them to control the muscles in one leg than in two legs. The pose may also keep the birds warmer when standing in cold water. When walking, a flamingo's legs appear to bend backward. This appearance is due to the fact that the joint midway up a flamingo's legs is the ankle, not the knee.

Unlike with a human, a flamingo's muscles get less tired when standing on one leg than on two. With little effort, a flamingo is able to "lock" its leg joints to stay motionless.

GREATER FLAMINGO

Phoenicopterus roseus

Length: 1.1 to 1.5 m (3.6 to 4.9 ft) tall
Range: Africa, southern Europe, and southern Asia
Habitat: Mudflats and coastal lagoons
Diet: Shrimp, seeds, mollusks, and tiny algae (plant-like living things)
Conservation: Not at risk

Greater flamingo

Flamingos suck water through their hooked beak, which has comb-like structures along its edges. These hold in bits of food but let water drain away.

American flamingos live in Central America, the Caribbean, and northern South America.

Flamingos are pink because of colored substances called carotenoids in the shrimp and plants they eat. Humans get a similar effect from eating too many carrots.

DID YOU KNOW? Flamingo parents feed their young chicks with "crop milk," a goo made by glands in the birds' throat, which they spit up.

Herons and Relatives

Herons, spoonbills, and the hamerkop are large wading birds with long legs and beaks. They live around the edges of oceans or freshwater. They have four toes, with three pointing forward and one backward. The toes are long, with a little webbing between them, to prevent the birds sinking into mud.

The Goliath Heron

The largest heron, the Goliath stands up to 1.5 m (5 ft) tall and has a wingspan, from wingtip to wingtip, of 2.3 m (7.5 ft). It is found in Africa, around coral reefs, mangrove forests, lakes, and swamps. When hunting, the Goliath usually stands completely still in shallow water. When a fish swims past, the bird spears it with an open beak, then swallows it whole.

The plumage of the Goliath heron's head and neck is chestnut colored.

The feathers' pink shade is gained from eating crustaceans that eat lots of red algae.

DID YOU KNOW? A spoonbill's nostrils are at the base of its beak, close to its eyes, so it can breathe when its beak is underwater during hunting.

The Hamerkop

This African bird hunts for fish, frogs, and shrimp in shallow water. It is found around saltwater, including mangrove forests, as well as freshwater. The only species in its family, the hamerkop is unusual for a wader because it spends a lot of time building giant stick nests in trees, often above water. Nests take up to 14 weeks to construct and can reach 1.5 m (5 ft) across.

Hamerkops build far more nests than they need, up to five per year.

Hamerkops often stand on top of one another, perhaps as a way of forming bonds within their flock.

To catch invertebrates, the bird swings its flat and spoon-shaped beak from side to side while wading through shallow water.

The roseate spoonbill lives around coasts and freshwater in the tropical and subtropical Americas.

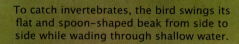

TRICOLORED HERON
Egretta tricolor

Length: 56 to 76 cm (22 to 30 in)
Range: Coasts of the Americas, from the northeastern United States to Brazil
Habitat: Mangrove forests, bays, and coastal marshes
Diet: Fish, amphibians, crustaceans, and insects
Conservation: Not at risk

Tricolored heron

Larids

Gulls, skimmers, and skuas are members of the Lari suborder. They are large seabirds that pluck fish from the ocean surface. These bold birds are also known to attack other birds, snatching their food and stealing eggs. Some have adapted to living inland and taking food wherever they find it, including rubbish tips.

Kleptoparasitism

Kleptoparasitism is when an animal eats the food that another animal has caught. Most gulls and skuas steal from other seabirds, either from time to time or, in the case of the great skua, as a main feeding method. The kleptoparasite attacks the other bird—using its own strength, large size, and sharp beak—until it drops its catch. Gulls do not stop at stealing from other birds: some swoop on humans' food, particularly takeaway food eaten on the beach.

A laughing gull is trying to force a white ibis to drop its fish. This gull eats anything it can find, from fish and mollusks to insects, eggs, chicks, and human food waste.

Skimmers

Skimmers have an unusual beak shape, with the lower jaw longer than the upper. This allows them to hunt by flying low over the water, with their beak slightly open. As the beak skims the water surface, the bird snatches up any small fish that are not quick enough to dart away.

Measuring up to 50 cm (20 in) long, the black skimmer hunts in the coastal waters of the Americas, as well as in rivers and lakes.

This gull has a wingspan of up to 1.2 m (4 ft).

The Heermann's gull watches brown pelicans as they hunt, then swoops to steal fish from their throat pouch.

The brown pelican scoops fish and water into its throat pouch. While it drains the water before swallowing, it is at risk from kleptoparasites.

A great skua feeds on an Arctic tern.

GREAT SKUA

Stercorarius skua

Length: 50 to 58 cm (20 to 23 in)
Range: Northern Atlantic Ocean
Habitat: Open ocean; nests on coasts and islands
Diet: Fish, birds, eggs, mice, rabbits, berries, and dead animals
Conservation: Not at risk

DID YOU KNOW? A herring gull was spotted using bits of bread as bait to catch goldfish in a pond in Paris, France.

Tubenoses

Albatrosses, petrels, and shearwaters are tubenoses, named for their beak shape. These seabirds have three webbed toes for paddling in the water, and many have wide wings for flying great distances over the ocean in search of fish. They nest in large groups, called colonies, often on remote islands.

Tube Nostrils

Tubenoses have large tube-shaped nostrils on the top or sides of their beak. These help to give the birds a very good sense of smell, which they use for finding prey and their home colony. In addition, tubenose beaks are covered in horny plates and hooked at the tip. Like other seabirds, tubenoses have a salt gland above their eyes. This gets rid of the salt they take in while swimming and eating. The gland releases salty liquid, which exits through the nostrils and drips down a groove in the beak.

Saltwater is dripping from the beak of this southern giant petrel.

Diving Petrels

Most tubenoses pluck prey from the water surface, but the diving petrels make dives of up to 80 m (260 ft) underwater. Unlike their relatives, diving petrels are small with short wings, so they feed close to shore instead of making long flights. When diving, they half-fold their wings, using them as paddles.

Like other diving petrels, the South Georgia diving petrel flies low over the waves, its feet just touching the surface, making it look like it is walking on water. Petrels are named after St Peter, who was said to walk on water.

DID YOU KNOW? The snowy albatross has the largest wingspan of any bird, reaching 3.7 m (12.1 ft) wide.

SNOWY ALBATROSS

Diomedea exulans

Length: 107 to 135 cm (42 to 53 in)
Range: Southern Ocean and southern Atlantic, Indian, and Pacific Oceans
Habitat: Open ocean; nests on islands
Diet: Squid, fish, crustaceans, and waste from ships
Conservation: Population shrinking due to tangling in fishing lines and pollution

Snowy albatross

The pillar-like nest is built from mud.

The black-browed albatross has smaller nostril tubes, on either side of its beak, than some of its relatives.

Just one egg is laid per year. The chick stays in the nest for around four months.

Gannets and Relatives

Gannets, boobies, cormorants, and frigatebirds are members of the Suliformes order. They are medium to large birds with hooked or cone-shaped beaks. All four of their toes are fully webbed. Apart from frigatebirds, which snatch fish from the water surface, these birds are expert underwater divers.

> Found only on the Galápagos Islands, the flightless cormorant has evolved to be such a good swimmer that it has lost the ability to fly.

Diving Styles

Cormorants dive from the water surface, swimming to depths of up to 45 m (150 ft) using their strong, webbed feet. Gannets and boobies are plunge divers, dropping into the water from a height. For this reason, they do not have nostrils on the outside of their beak, which would fill with water as they crashed into the ocean. Instead, they breathe through their mouth. They also have air sacs in their face and chest, which act like cushions.

The northern gannet plunge dives from heights of up to 45 m (150 ft), reaching 100 km/h (62 mph) as it hits the water.

RED-FOOTED BOOBY
Sula sula

Length: 65 to 75 cm (26 to 30 in)
Range: Tropical Atlantic, Indian, and Pacific Oceans
Habitat: Open ocean; nests on islands
Diet: Small fish and squid
Conservation: Not at risk

Red-footed booby

The cormorant propels itself through the water using its large feet and sturdy legs.

The wings are far too small to lift this large bird, up to 1 m (3.3 ft) long, off the ground.

Frigatebirds

There are five species of frigatebirds, which live around tropical and subtropical oceans. During mating season, frigatebirds cluster on remote islands in colonies of up to 5,000 birds. The males of all species have a bright red throat pouch. To attract females, the males inflate their throat pouch, lift their head, and open and shake their wings.

This male great frigatebird is hoping to attract a female.

DID YOU KNOW? "Booby" comes from the Spanish slang word *bobo*, meaning silly, as these birds often landed on sailing ships and were quickly eaten by sailors.

225

Sea Ducks

Although most people think of ducks as freshwater birds, more than 20 species spend part of their year in coastal seas. Ducks have broad, rounded bodies that float easily at the water surface, webbed feet, and strong legs for paddling.

Diving Ducks

Many freshwater ducks feed by tipping themselves up in shallow water, reaching to the bottom with their tails in the air. These "dabbling" ducks mostly feed on water plants. In contrast, most sea ducks are divers, able to swim to the bottom of deep water to prey on water creatures. Diving ducks usually have bigger feet, set farther back on their body, than dabblers, making them waddle awkwardly on land.

The common eider dives for mussels, which it swallows whole. The shells are crushed in a muscly part of the stomach called the gizzard.

The common scoter spends its winters along the coasts of the northern Atlantic Ocean.

Useful Beaks

Like all birds, ducks do not have teeth, so they swallow their food whole. Their strong beak and jaw allow them to tear off plants or grapple with prey. A duck's beak shape is suited to its diet. Scoter ducks have large, broad beaks for poking in mud and grasping hard-shelled crustaceans and mollusks. The mergansers are fish-eaters, with jagged edges to their long, thin beaks, which helps them grasp their slippery prey.

The red-breasted merganser hunts for small salmon and trout.

This bird is often found on coastal mudflats.

The three front toes are connected by webbing, while the fourth, back toe is very small.

This male common shelduck has a bright red beak, which it uses to dig for mollusks, crustaceans, and insects.

SPECTACLED EIDER
Somateria fischeri

Length: 52 to 57 cm (20 to 22 in)
Range: Arctic and northern Pacific Oceans
Habitat: Open ocean and coastal waters; nests on wetlands
Diet: Mollusks, crustaceans, insects, grasses, and berries
Conservation: Population shrinking due to climate change

Spectacled eider

DID YOU KNOW? In the past, eider ducks were hunted for the layer of very soft, thick "down" feathers next to their skin, which were used to make eiderdowns.

Puffins and Relatives

Puffins are members of the auk family, along with the guillemots, murres, and auklets. These seabirds are high-speed underwater divers, using their wings as paddles. In the air, they have to flap their short wings very quickly to stay aloft. On land, they are clumsy walkers, with an upright penguin-like posture.

Both male and female tufted puffins grow long tufts of feathers as mating season approaches.

Egg Laying

Birds in the auk family spend most of their life far out to sea, but they go ashore during the mating season, when they gather in colonies along the coast. They often return to the same mate year after year, laying just one egg per year. Most species nest on cliff ledges or in rock clefts, where their egg is out of reach from predators.

The thick-billed murre lays its egg on a cliff ledge. The egg is pointed at one end, which means it rolls in a circle rather than off the ledge.

PARAKEET AUKLET
Aethia psittacula

Length: 23 to 26 cm (9 to 10 in)
Range: Northern Pacific Ocean
Habitat: Open ocean; nests on rocky islands
Diet: Jellyfish, crustaceans, and small fish
Conservation: Population shrinking on some islands due to accidental introduction of rats

Parakeet auklet

DID YOU KNOW? By around 1852, the great auk had been driven to extinction by human hunters who wanted its soft feathers, eggs, and meat.

After the mating season ends, the bright red feet will fade.

With short wings but a stocky body, the puffin finds takeoff easiest when it launches into the air from a high cliff.

Deft Divers

Auks need to move fast underwater to capture the quickly swimming fish that are usually their food, including cod, herring, and sandeel. The birds must hold their breath throughout a dive, so they angle their streamlined body to descend to their desired depth as swiftly as possible, then use up and down wing strokes to change direction as they pursue their prey.

The common murre can dive to depths of 180 m (590 ft), never staying underwater for more than 200 seconds.

229

Penguins

A penguin's small wings, which are shaped like a dolphin's flippers, cannot lift it into the air at all. These seabirds spend three-quarters of their life swimming in the ocean, with most species living in the cold waters of the southern hemisphere. Their blubber and thick, waterproof feathers keep them warm.

Hunters

Penguins dive for fish, squid, and krill. The largest species, such as the 110 cm/43 in-tall emperor penguin, can dive as deep as 565 m (1,855 ft) and stay underwater for up to 22 minutes. Smaller species, such as the little penguin that is only 33 cm (13 in) tall, cannot swim as fast or hold their breath so long, and find their food near the surface. All penguins catch prey in their beak and swallow it whole as they swim.

When the gentoo penguin is swimming, its movements look similar to a bird flying through the air. When the gentoo comes ashore, it is on Antarctica or islands in the far southern seas.

Getting Together

Penguins are sociable birds: they hunt, sleep on the water surface, and nest with other penguins. Many species come to land only to mate, when they gather in large and loud colonies. Penguins often return to the same mate year after year. However, females desert their mate if he no longer seems healthy. A large body size, a deep call, and bright feathers are signs of fitness. In most species, males and females share the exhausting care of their eggs and young chicks.

The world's largest penguin colony is on Zavodovskiy Island, in the Southern Ocean. It is home to 1.2 million chinstrap (pictured) and macaroni penguins.

230

Up to 1 m (3.3 ft) tall, the king penguin gathers to mate on islands in the cold southern oceans.

Parents take turns warming their egg, balancing it on their feet and tucked inside a pouch of skin.

Most penguins lay two eggs, but the king penguin lays only one, which takes 55 days to hatch.

SOUTHERN ROCKHOPPER PENGUIN

Eudyptes chrysocome

Length: 45 to 58 cm (18 to 23 in)
Range: Southern Atlantic, Indian, and Pacific Oceans
Habitat: Open ocean; nests on rocky islands and coasts
Diet: Krill, fish, squid, and octopus
Conservation: Population shrinking due to climate change, overfishing, and oil spills

Southern rockhopper penguin

DID YOU KNOW? The Galápagos penguin is the only penguin that does not live in the southern hemisphere, as its island home straddles the equator.

Chapter 10: Invertebrates

Anthozoa

Anthozoa include sea anemones and corals, as well as sea pens, fans, and whips. Corals are in two main groups: the soft corals and the stony corals, which build the hard skeletons that form coral reefs. Apart from sea anemones, which live alone, most anthozoans live in groups called colonies.

Life Cycle

Adult anthozoans are called polyps. They are tube-shaped, with a central mouth surrounded by tentacles for grabbing prey. For anthozoans that live alone, each polyp attaches to the seafloor with its foot. For anthozoans that live in colonies, the foot attaches to other, identical polyps. Young anthozoans, called larvae, have simpler body shapes. They swim along till they are ready to settle down and grow into adults.

A sea fan is a colony of thousands of tiny polyps, each with eight tentacles.

Sea Anemones

A sea anemone polyp has tens or hundreds of tentacles, which are armed with stinging cells. If the cells are touched, they shoot out an arrow-like structure that sticks into the prey or predator, injecting them with venom. The venom paralyzes prey, so it can be moved easily to the anenome's mouth.

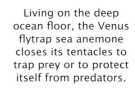

Living on the deep ocean floor, the Venus flytrap sea anemone closes its tentacles to trap prey or to protect itself from predators.

The common clownfish lives among the tentacles of carpet sea anemones, where it is well-hidden from predators.

The anemone benefits from hosting clownfish because they scare away other fish, such as butterflyfish, that would nibble their tentacles.

Clownfish are covered in thick mucus that protects them from anemone stings.

SHORT-QUILL SEA PEN
Virgularia gustaviana

Length: 30 to 40 cm (12 to 16 in)
Range: Tropical Indian and Pacific Oceans
Habitat: Sandy or muddy seabed in shallow, coastal waters
Diet: Plankton
Conservation: Not at risk

A short-quill sea pen colony is symmetrical.

DID YOU KNOW? There are more than 6,000 species of anthozoans, ranging from single polyps just 1 cm (0.4 in) across to colonies more than 1 m (3.3 ft) across.

Jellyfish

Despite their name, jellyfish are not fish but invertebrates related to anthozoans. Adult jellyfish have soft bodies with an umbrella-shaped "bell" and long tentacles. They swim by expanding and squeezing their bell, pushing water behind them.

The golden jellyfish lives only in Jellyfish Lake, on the island of Eil Malk in the Pacific Ocean.

Changing Body

A jellyfish starts life as a tiny, floating larva. When the larva finds a rock or other surface, it attaches to it and starts to grow into a polyp. Jellyfish polyps look like anthozoan polyps, with a central mouth and tentacles for catching prey. After a few weeks or months, the polyp starts budding: its body breaks off into baby jellyfish, which swim away. These grow into adult jellyfish, called medusae. Medusae release eggs that grow into larvae.

The bell of a lion's mane jellyfish medusa can grow as wide as 2.3 m (7.5 ft).

Stinging Tentacles

Jellyfish tentacles have stinging cells that can stun or kill prey. Jellyfish may catch prey by trailing their tentacles behind them or sinking through the water with their tentacles spread wide. When prey is within reach, the tentacles direct it to the mouth, in the centre of the bell.

The moon jellyfish uses its tentacles to catch zooplankton.

The seawater lake is connected to the ocean by tunnels.

Thousands of golden jellyfish swim across the lake together every day.

Crowned jellyfish

CROWNED JELLYFISH

Cephea cephea

Length: 75 to 85 cm (30 to 33 in)

Range: Tropical Atlantic, Indian, and Pacific Oceans

Habitat: Open ocean

Diet: Plankton, algae, shrimp, and eggs

Conservation: Not at risk

DID YOU KNOW? Jellyfish do not have eyes or a brain, but they respond to messages from their nerves, which sense touch and heat.

Octopus and Squid

> The blue-ringed octopus lives in rock pools and coral reefs in the tropical Pacific and Indian Oceans.

Octopus and squid are cephalopods, a group of 800 species that also includes nautilus and cuttlefish. Cephalopods have large heads and eyes, as well as arms or tentacles. Most of them have an ink sac, which can release a cloud of dark ink to confuse predators.

Moving Along

Octopus have eight arms covered with suckers, which they use to hold prey. Squid also have eight suckered arms, plus two long tentacles for grabbing. Octopus and squid can swim very fast by sucking in water, then pushing it out through a tube-shaped body part called a siphon. The animal moves in the opposite direction to the jet of water. Octopus can also crawl along the seafloor, while squid can swim gently by waving their fins.

The bigfin reef squid's skin is covered in color-changing cells. It uses these to control its body color and pattern.

Intelligent Invertebrates

Cephalopods have large brains and are the most intelligent of all invertebrates. They show this through a number of skills. Some octopus signal to each other by changing their body color, while Humboldt squid work together to capture prey. Several species of octopus, including blue-ringed octopus, use rocks and other objects to build dens.

SOUTHERN BOBTAIL SQUID

Euprymna tasmanica

Length: 6 to 7 cm (2.4 to 2.8 in)
Range: Temperate coasts of Australia
Habitat: Seagrass meadows and sandy or muddy seafloors in shallow water
Diet: Shrimp and fish
Conservation: Not known

The southern bobtail squid is bioluminescent.

When the octopus feels threatened, the rings on its skin turn bright blue to frighten away predators.

This coconut octopus is walking on two "legs" as it carries a shell to hide inside.

Although all octopus have a venomous bite, only blue-ringed octopus make a venom so deadly it can kill humans.

DID YOU KNOW? The smallest cephalopods are pygmy squid, which grow little more than 1 cm (0.4 in) long.

237

Crabs

Crabs belong to a group of arthropods called crustaceans. Like all arthropods, including insects and spiders, they have a tough exoskeleton and jointed legs, which bend easily for walking. Unlike other arthropods, crustaceans have two pairs of feelers, called antennae, on their heads.

Ten Legs

Crabs have five pairs of legs. The back four pairs are for walking, often in a sideways direction because of their position and joints, but sometimes forward or backward. The front pair of legs, often called claws, end in pincers. The claws are used for grabbing and killing prey, as well as for signalling and fighting.

Male fiddler crabs have one claw much larger than the other. They use it for signalling to females and for fighting off other males so they can win a mate.

Hermit Crabs

Although hermit crabs are crustaceans, they are not true crabs. True crabs have a very tough shell covering their body, called a carapace. Hermit crabs do not have a carapace, so they protect their soft body using the empty shell of another creature, often a sea snail.

Hermit crabs carry around an abandoned seashell, then pull their whole body inside at the first sign of danger.

HALLOWEEN CRAB

Gecarcinus quadratus

Length: 10 to 12 cm (4 to 4.7 in)
Range: Pacific coast of Central America
Habitat: Mangrove forest, sand dunes, coastal rainforest, and shallow ocean
Diet: Leaves and young plants
Conservation: Not at risk

Halloween crab

The red rock crab lives on rocky seashores in Central and South America.

The carapace is around 8 cm (3 in) long.

Like other beach-living crabs, the female red rock crab releases her larvae into the water. When the larvae have grown into adults, they swim ashore.

DID YOU KNOW? The largest crab is the Japanese spider crab, which reaches 3.8 m (12 ft) from pincer to pincer but has a carapace only 0.4 m (1.3 ft) wide.

Lobsters and Relatives

Lobsters, shrimps, and prawns are all crustaceans with ten legs. In addition to their legs, they have several other pairs of appendages, or long body parts, including antennae and mouthparts. All these crustaceans have bodies that are segmented, or divided into parts.

Found on coral reefs in the Indian and Pacific Oceans, the harlequin shrimp feeds on starfish.

Clawed Lobsters

True lobsters have claws on their first three pairs of legs, with the front pair having the biggest claws of all. They spend their life on the seafloor, hiding in crevices or burrows and coming out to catch fish, molluscs, and worms. Although lobsters have eyes, which are usually on stalks, it is murky on the seafloor, so they hunt by using their antennae to sense the chemical "smells" given off by prey.

Sometimes weighing more than 20 kg (44 lb), the American lobster is the world's heaviest crustacean.

Spiny Lobsters

Spiny lobsters, which are clawless, have thick and spiny antennae. These antennae play a special role during migration. Every autumn, groups of Caribbean and California spiny lobsters walk across the seafloor from cold and stormy shallow waters into warm and calm deeper waters. The lobsters walk one behind the other, draping their antennae over the lobster in front.

Migrating around 40 km (25 miles), Caribbean spiny lobsters form a line to make pushing through the water easier for all the lobsters except the leader.

240

PINK SHRIMP

Pandalus montagui

Length: 4 to 5 cm (1.6 to 2 in)
Range: Arctic Ocean and northern Atlantic Ocean
Habitat: Ocean floor at depths of 20 to 100 m (65 to 330 ft)
Diet: Small invertebrates such as crustaceans and worms
Conservation: Not at risk

Pink shrimp

The petal-like antennae are used for "smelling" prey.

The harlequin shrimp's eyes are on short stalks.

These large, flat claws are used for attracting a mate.

DID YOU KNOW? As they grow, crustaceans must shed their exoskeleton, then grow a new one, to make room for their larger body.

241

Bivalves

Bivalves are soft-bodied animals that live in a tough shell. The shell is in two halves joined by a hinge, so it can open and close. Bivalves include clams, cockles, mussels, and oysters. Many bivalves bury themselves in the sand or mud of the seafloor, while others attach to rocks.

Filter Feeders

Most bivalves eat tiny algae and other small living things using a method called filter feeding. Water is sucked inside the shell, often through a tube called the "inhalant siphon." The water passes through the bivalve's gills, which are covered in sticky mucus. Bits of food stick to the mucus. The used water is pumped out, often through another tube, the "exhalant siphon."

This cockle has stuck out its pink foot, which it uses for burrowing into the seabed. It can also jump by bending and straightening its foot.

Making Pearls

Bivalves make their own shells, using a mineral called calcium carbonate. Some oysters and mussels make a form of calcium carbonate called nacre, which is iridescent, or shines in the shades of the rainbow. They also make pearls out of the same material. When a grain of sand or tiny parasite enters their shell, the bivalve surrounds the intruder with layers of nacre, forming a pearl.

A pearl oyster has lined its shell and made a pearl from iridescent nacre.

DID YOU KNOW? The world's largest pearl, formed inside a giant clam, measures 67 cm (26 in) long and weighs 34 kg (75 lb).

FLAME SCALLOP

Ctenoides scaber

Length: 6 to 8 cm (2.4 to 3.1 in)
Range: Caribbean Sea, in the Atlantic Ocean
Habitat: Seafloor on coral reefs
Diet: Phytoplankton
Conservation: Not at risk

Flame scallop

Giant clams live on coral reefs in the Indian and Pacific Oceans.

Giant clams can measure as much as 137 cm (54 in) across and live for over 100 years.

After filter feeding on plankton, the clam pumps out used water through the exhalant siphon.

243

Sea Slugs and Snails

Slugs and snails are gastropods. They have a head, with two or four tentacles equipped with eyes, and a long foot, which they use to crawl over the seafloor or ground. Around half of the 60,000 species of gastropods live in oceans, while the rest live in freshwater or on land.

Shell or No Shell

Gastropods with a shell are usually called snails, while those without a shell are called slugs. Sea snails are often given names like cowry, conch, limpet, and periwinkle. Their shell usually has a spiral shape and is large enough for the animal to pull its whole body inside for protection. Sea slugs are often called nudibranchs.

This purple-lined nudibranch lives on coral reefs in the tropical Indian and Pacific Oceans.

The tulip snail crawls over the seabed in search of bivalves or other molluscs to attack with its radula, which is a long tongue covered in tiny teeth. The radula is sharp enough to bore through shells.

FLAMINGO TONGUE SNAIL

Cyphoma gibbosum

Length: 1.8 to 4.4 cm (0.7 to 1.7 in)
Range: Tropical western Atlantic Ocean
Habitat: Soft corals in shallow water
Diet: Soft corals
Conservation: Population shrinking due to capture by tourists

The flamingo tongue snail covers its shell with flaps of patterned body tissue.

DID YOU KNOW? Nudibranchs are hermaphrodites, which means they have both male and female body parts, but they still have to find another nudibranch to mate with.

The nudibranch takes oxygen from the water through its frondy gills.

The tentacles are sensitive to touch, taste, and smell.

Nudibranchs

Since nudibranchs do not have a shell, they have evolved other methods of protection. Many nudibranchs eat stinging or bad-tasting animals, such as sea anemones and sponges. Without harming themselves, these nudibranchs store their prey's nasty chemicals in their own bodies. Some nudibranchs can make their own bad-tasting chemicals. If a predator makes the mistake of eating a nudibranch, they will remember not to do it again.

The opalescent nudibranch feeds on stinging sea anemones. Its bright pattern acts as a warning sign to predators that it is bad to eat.

Starfish

Also known as sea stars, starfish live on the ocean floor, from the shore to the depths. They are radially symmetrical, which means they usually have five equal parts arranged around their centre, like slices of a pie. Although most starfish have five arms, some have over fifty.

Creeping Predators

Starfish prey on other seafloor animals, particularly invertebrates. The starfish's mouth is in the middle of its underside. Many starfish can hunt prey much larger than their mouth. When they find prey, they move on top of it and push their stomach out through their mouth, inside-out. The stomach makes digestive fluids to break down the prey. After a while, the stomach and the partly digested prey are pulled inside.

This crown-of-thorns starfish has climbed onto coral and stuck out its stomach. It is turning the coral polyps to mush.

Tube Feet

The undersides of a starfish's arms have many tube-shaped growths called tube feet. Starfish creep slowly across the seafloor by waving their tube feet, which stick to surfaces, with one part of an arm attaching to a surface as another lets go.

The ochre starfish is often seen on wave-washed rocks. As well as being used for movement, its strong tube feet can open the shells of bivalves.

COMMON SUNSTAR

Crossaster papposus

Length: 20 to 35 cm (8 to 14 in)
Range: Arctic and northern Atlantic and Pacific Oceans
Habitat: Rocky seafloor from shore rock pools to depths of 300 m (985 ft)
Diet: Starfish, sea urchins, bivalves, and sea squirts
Conservation: Population shrinking due to global warming

Common sunstar

Found in shallow waters of the Indian and Pacific Oceans, the red knob starfish grows to about 30 cm (12 in) wide.

If it loses one of its arms, this starfish can slowly grow a new one.

At the tip of each arm is an eyespot, which allows the starfish to see light and dark shapes.

DID YOU KNOW? A single crown-of-thorns starfish can eat up to 6 sq m (65 sq ft) of coral reef every year.

247

Sea Cucumbers and Urchins

Like their relatives the starfish, sea cucumbers and sea urchins are echinoderms. The 7,000 members of this group are found only in the oceans, usually on the seafloor. Adult echinoderms are radially symmetrical and have tough, often spiny, skin.

Sea Cucumbers

Named for their cucumber-shaped body, these echinoderms have a mouth surrounded by tentacles at one end, so—unlike starfish and urchins—they are usually seen lying on their side. They use their tentacles for catching plankton or digging in sand and mud for waste to eat. While most sea cucumbers crawl across the seafloor on their tube feet, some can push themselves off the bottom and float along.

The red-lined sea cucumber has many hard spikes for protection. When threatened, it curls into a ball.

Sea Urchins

These round and spiny echinoderms live on the seafloor, from rock pools to 5,000 m (16,000 ft) deep. Some sea urchins have venomous spines. Like all echinoderms, they do not have a brain, but they have nerves that are sensitive to touch, light, and chemical "smells" in the water. When one of their spines is touched, all the spines move to point at the predator.

Smelling algae to eat, these red and purple sea urchins have crawled across the rock on their tube feet.

248

CHOCOLATE CHIP SEA CUCUMBER

Isostichopus badionotus

Length: 15 to 45 cm (6 to 18 in)
Range: Tropical and subtropical Atlantic Ocean
Habitat: Seafloor from 0 to 55 m (180 ft)
Diet: Waste materials on the seafloor
Conservation: Not at risk

Chocolate chip sea cucumber

With spikes up to 10 cm (4 in) long, the slate pencil sea urchin lives on coral reefs in the Indian and Pacific Oceans.

The slate pencil can crawl as much as 1 m (3.3 ft) per day in search of algae to eat.

On the underside of the urchin's body is its mouth, armed with teeth for scraping and biting.

DID YOU KNOW? The longest sea cucumber is the tiger tail, which lives on coral reefs in the Atlantic Ocean and reaches 2 m (6.6 ft) long.

249

Worms

We call invertebrates "worms" when they have a long body and no limbs. Although worms share this basic shape, they belong to several different groups that are not closely related to each other, including flatworms, ribbon worms, and annelid worms, which have bodies divided into segments.

Growing up to 8 cm (3 in) long, this feather duster worm lives among coral reefs and rocks in the tropical Indian and Pacific Oceans.

Sessile Worms

Sessile means "fixed in one place." Sessile worms attach themselves to the seafloor, rock, or coral, then build a hard tube around their soft body. Most of them build this tube from a tough mineral that they make in their own body, but some make tubes from mud or sand.

The Christmas tree worm is a sessile annelid worm. It extends two spiral mouthparts from its mineral tube. These mouthparts are covered in feathery tentacles for trapping bits of food.

Bristleworms

There are around 10,000 species of bristleworms, which are annelids. Many bristleworms crawl over the seabed, but some are burrowers, swimmers, or sessile. A few live on land or inside other creatures. Each of a bristleworm's body segments has a pair of paddle-like parapodia (meaning "beside feet"), which are used for movement. The parapodia are covered in bristles, which—in some species—can give a venomous sting.

A species of bristleworm, the bearded fireworm feeds on corals, anemones, and small crustaceans.

As tiny living things float past, the feathery tentacles catch them, sending the food down grooves to the central mouth.

This sessile worm's tube is built from sand and mud stuck together with the worm's own mucus.

BOBBIT WORM

Eunice aphroditois

Length: 0.5 to 3 m (1.6 to 10 ft)

Range: Tropical and subtropical Atlantic, Indian, and Pacific Oceans

Habitat: Gravel, mud, or coral seafloor between 10 and 40 m (30 and 130 ft)

Diet: Small fish, invertebrates, and seaweed

Conservation: Not at risk

The Bobbit worm buries itself while waiting for prey.

DID YOU KNOW? If part of the banded nemertean ribbon worm is broken off, it grows into a new worm—200,000 worms can grow from one adult.

251

Glossary

AGGREGATION
A gathering of living things, often at a particular time of year or place.

ALGAE
Simple plantlike living things that usually live in and around water, such as seaweeds.

AMPULLAE OF LORENZINI
Organs—found in sharks, rays, and chimaeras—that can detect the electric fields made by animals' muscles as they move.

ANAL FIN
A fin on a fish's underside, toward the tail.

ANTENNA
A slender "feeler" found on the head of some invertebrates.

APPENDAGE
A body part that extends from the body or head, such as an antenna.

ARTHROPOD
An invertebrate with a hard covering, or exoskeleton, and jointed legs, such as a crab.

ATOM
The smallest portion of any material that can exist on its own.

BACTERIA
Microscopic living things with one simple cell.

BARBEL
A whisker-like body part on the snout which helps fish to taste and smell prey.

BIOLUMINESCENT
Able to make its own light.

BIVALVE
A soft-bodied invertebrate that lives in a hinged two-part shell, such as a clam or mussel.

BLOOD VESSEL
A tube that carries blood through an animal's body.

BLUBBER
A thick layer of fat, found in water-dwelling mammals and penguins, which keeps the animal warm.

CAMOUFLAGE
The way the shade, pattern, and shape of an animal make it less visible in its habitat.

CARTILAGE
A body material that is strong, bendy, and lightweight.

CAUDAL FIN
The tail fin.

CELL
The smallest working part of a living thing.

CEPHALOFOIL
The outward extensions of the head of a shark in the hammerhead family.

CETACEAN
A water-living mammal with a streamlined body and two flippers: a whale, dolphin, or porpoise.

CHIMAERA
A fish with a skeleton made of cartilage, bare skin, and a single, covered gill opening.

CLASS
A scientific group that includes animals with the same body plan, such as bony-skeletoned or cartilaginous fish.

COLONY
A group of animals living together.

CORAL REEF
An underwater structure made by groups of tiny animals, named coral polyps, that build hard skeletons around their soft bodies.

COUNTERSHADING
A form of camouflage in which an animal is darker on its upperside and paler on its underside, making it harder to spot when viewed from above or below in sunlit water.

CRITICALLY ENDANGERED
Describes a species that is at extremely high risk of becoming extinct soon.

CRUSTACEAN
An arthropod with two pairs of antennae on its head, such as a crab.

CURRENT
A stream of water that flows through the ocean.

CYANOBACTERIA
Bacteria that make their own food from sunlight.

DERMAL DENTICLE
A pointed scale found on the skin of sharks and most rays, with a similar structure to teeth.

DIATOM
A microscopic, single-celled living thing that makes its own food from sunlight.

DORSAL FIN
A fin on the upper side of a fish, with sharks having one or two.

ELECTRIC FIELD
An area around an electric charge in which its force can be felt.

ENDANGERED
Describes a species that is likely to become extinct in the near future.

ESTUARY
The mouth of a large river, where it meets the ocean.

EVOLVE
To change gradually over time.

EXOSKELETON
The hard outer covering of some invertebrates.

FAMILY
A scientific group that includes genera similar to each other.

FILTER FEEDING
Straining food from the water using comb- or net-like mouthparts.

FIN
A body part that juts from the body of fish and some other water-living animals, helping them swim.

FISH
A water-living animal that takes oxygen from the water using gills and usually has fins.

FRESH WATER
Unsalted water, such as rivers, lakes, and ponds.

GENUS (PLURAL GENERA)
A scientific group that includes species very similar to each other.

GILL
An organ in fish that takes oxygen from water.

GILL SLIT
An uncovered opening to a gill that can be seen in sharks and rays.

GLAND
A body part that makes a substance for use in the body or for release.

GLOBAL WARMING
Rising world temperatures caused mainly by human activities.

HABITAT
The natural home of an animal, plant, or other living thing.

HEMISPHERE
Half of the planet, such as the northern or southern half on either side of the equator.

INTERTIDAL ZONE
The area on the shore that is below water during high tides and above water when the sea draws out.

INVERTEBRATE
An animal without a backbone, such as a crab, squid, or insect.

LARVA
A young stage in the life cycle of some animals, during which the animal looks very different from its adult form.

LEAST CONCERN
Describes a species that is not currently at risk of extinction.

LOBE
A division of a body part, such as the upper and lower portions of a caudal fin.

MAMMAL
An animal that grows hair at some point in its life and feeds its young on milk, such as a whale or human.

MARINE
Found in the ocean.

MATE
A male or female partner for making babies.

MICROORGANISM
A living thing that is so small it can be seen only with a microscope.

MIGRATION
A seasonal or daily movement of animals from one region to another.

MINERAL
A solid that forms in the ground or in water.

MOLLUSK
An invertebrate with a soft body and sometimes a hard shell, such as a slug, snail, clam, or octopus.

MUCUS
A slimy substance made by some animals.

MUDFLAT
Muddy land that is left uncovered when the sea draws out at low tide.

NEAR THREATENED
Describes a species that is likely to become endangered in the near future.

NICTITATING MEMBRANE
A third, see-through eyelid that protects a groundshark's eyeball.

ORDER
A scientific group that includes families similar to each other.

ORGAN
A body part that does a particular job, such as the heart or brain.

OVERFISHING
Catching so many of a particular species that it drops dramatically in number.

OXYGEN
A gas found in air and water which is needed by animals' cells to make energy to do their work.

PARASITE
A living thing that lives in or on another living thing.

PECTORAL FIN
One of a pair of fins on either side of a fish, behind its head.

PELVIC FIN
One of a pair of fins on a fish's underside, toward its tail.

PHOTOSYNTHESIS
The process of using sunlight to make food energy.

PHYTOPLANKTON
Tiny drifting plants, algae, and some bacteria that make food from sunlight.

PIGMENT
A substance that gives color.

POD
A group of cetaceans.

POLAR
In the cold regions around the North and South Pole, in the Arctic and Southern Oceans.

POLYP
The sessile, or non-moving, life stage of invertebrates such as corals.

PREDATOR
An animal that hunts other animals.

PREY
An animal that is killed by another animal for food.

PUPIL
The opening in an eye that lets in light. Light bounces off objects and into the eye, where it stimulates cells that message the brain.

RAY
A fish with a skeleton made of cartilage, a flattened body, five or six gill slits on its underside, and usually skin covered by dermal denticles.

REPTILE
An animal that usually lays eggs on land and has a dry scaly skin.

SCALE
A small, hard plate that protects the skin of most fish and reptiles.

SCHOOL
A group of fish.

SCLERA
The outer layer of the eye.

SEA
An area of saltwater smaller than an ocean that is partly or completely surrounded by land.

SEASONAL
Happening at a particular time of year.

SHARK
A fish with a skeleton made of cartilage, five to seven gill slits on the sides of its head, and skin covered by dermal denticles.

SNOUT
The part of an animal's head containing the nose and jaws.

SPECIES
A group of living things that look similar and can mate together.

SPIRACLE
Found in some sharks and rays, a hole behind each eye that lets water pass into the gills.

SUBARCTIC
In the cold area just to the south of the Arctic.

SUBSPECIES
A population of a species that lives in a particular area and differs from other populations of the species.

SUBTROPICAL
In the areas to the south or north of the tropics, where the ocean is fairly warm all year.

TEMPERATE
In the areas between the subtropics and polar regions, where the ocean ranges from cold to warm.

TENTACLE
A long, thin body part, used for feeling or grabbing.

THREATENED
At risk of extinction in the future.

TIDE
The rising and falling of the ocean at the shore, caused by the pull of the Moon's gravity on the water.

TROPICAL
In the area around the equator, where the water is warm all year.

TUBE FEET
Small tube-like appendages used by some invertebrates for movement.

VENOMOUS
Able to give a poisoned bite or sting.

VULNERABLE
Describes a species that is at risk of extinction in the medium term.

WETLANDS
Land that is partly covered by water, such as swamps and marshes.

WINGSPAN
The distance from wingtip to wingtip.

ZOOPLANKTON
Tiny animals and eggs that drift through the water.

Index

African manatee 197
albatross 7, 222, 223
algae 33, 36–7, 212
ambush predators 24, 38, 108, 152
American crocodile 210, 211
ampullae of Lorenzini 60, 61, 74, 132, 147, 150, 155, 158, 159, 167
angelsharks 62, 73, 146, 152–3
anglerfish 45, 184–5
angular roughshark 138–9
anthozoa 232–3
apex predators 22, 69, 114, 210
archerfish 34
Arctic Ocean 8, 42
Arctic tern 43
Atlantic Ocean 8, 9
Atlantic seal 205
Atlantic sixgill 52–3
Atlantic spotted dolphin 17
auk 228, 229
avocet 215

baleen whales 188–9, 190
bamboo sharks 102–8
banded houndshark 82–3
banded nemertean ribbon worm 251
banded wobbegong 54–5
barbels 61, 97, 98, 151
Bargibant's pygmy seahorse 172
barnacles 32
basking shark 63, 126, 128–9
beaches 30–1
beaked whale 190
beluga whale 190
bigeye tuna 29
billfish 182–3
bioluminescence 45, 143, 184
birds 7, 20–1, 214–31
  beaks 226
  diving 222, 224, 226, 229, 230
  endangered species 27
  kleptoparasitism 220
bivalves 32, 242–3
black-browed albatross 223
black-necked stilt 214
black prince copepod 22–3
blacktip reef shark 51, 92–3
blind shark 98–9
blubber 42, 43, 194, 202, 230
blue-ringed octopus 236–7
blue shark 60–1
blue whale 17, 22, 189
bobbit worm 251
bonnethead shark 76–7
bony fish 12, 13, 170–87
boobies 224, 225
bottlenose dolphin 193
bowhead whales 17, 43
bowmouth guitarfish 154–5
boxfish 174–5
bristleworms 250
brittle stars 36
broadnose sevengill shark 144–5
brownbanded bamboo shark 102–3, 108
bull sharks 88–9
bullhead sharks 73, 146–9

camouflage 25, 54, 102, 108, 115, 136, 170, 173
Caribbean reef shark 84–5
carnivores 16, 23
carpet sharks 73, 108–13
cartilage: cartilaginous fish 12, 154–69
  sharks 50
catsharks 79, 80–1
cephalofoil 74, 77

cephalopods 236–7
chimaeras 155, 168–9
chocolate chip sea cucumber 249
Chondrichthyes 154, 155
chromists 10, 11, 28
clams 242
climates, ocean 28
clown triggerfish 175
clownfish, common 233
cockles 242
conservation status 71
cookiecutter shark 62, 142–3
copper sharks 62–3
copperband butterfly fish 41
coral catshark 56–7
coral reefs 7, 40–1, 85, 92, 176, 178, 232, 247
cormorants 224–5
counterillumination 136
cow sharks 73, 144–5
crabs 31, 37, 238–9
crocodiles 18, 19, 210–11
crown-of-thorns starfish 247
crowned jellyfish 235
crustaceans 238–9
currents 9

daisy parrotfish 186
Dall's porpoise 195
damselfish 176
decorator crabs 37
deep ocean 44–5
defensive techniques 25
depths 28, 29
dermal denticles 54, 95, 106, 107, 139, 154, 157
devil ray 162
diatoms 11, 22
diving records 55, 198
dogfish sharks 73, 134–43
dolphins 24, 190, 192–3
dragonets 180–1
ducks, sea 226–7
dugong 196
dwarf lanternshark 51

eared seals 206–7
echinoderms 248–9
echolocation 190
eider ducks 227
electric rays 164–5
elephant seals 204
embryophagy 123
endangered species 26–7, 71, 118, 122, 131, 138, 158, 193, 194, 208
epaulette shark 104–5
Eurasian otter 200
exoskeletons 241
eyespots 104, 166

feather duster worm 250–1
filter feeding 63, 94, 126, 242, 243
fish 12–13, 41
  bony fish 170–87
  brain size 48
  cartilaginous fish 154–69
  classes 12, 154
  deep-sea 44, 45
  early fish 154
  endangered 154, 158, 159
  fish nurseries 35, 38
  mega-shoals 24
  polar fish 42
  records 13, 162, 172, 175, 182, 184
  see also individual species
fishing 26, 70, 131, 135
  overfishing 26, 27, 43, 70, 71, 118, 131, 158, 231
flame scallop 243
flamingo tongue snail 244
flamingos 216–17
flatback turtle 209
flatfish 170–1
flightless cormorant 224–5

floral blenny 39
flounder 170–1
food chains 22–3
fossils 14, 68, 169
frigatebird 224, 225
frilled sharks 73, 144–5
frogfish 184–5
fur seals 206–7

Galápagos penguin 231
Galápagos shark 6–7
gannets 224–5
gastropods 244–5
giant clams 243
giant oceanic manta ray 162
giant tube worms 46, 47
glycoprotein 42
goblin shark 132–3
golden jellyfish 234–5
Goliath heron 218
Gorgona guitarfish 156–7
Great Barrier Reef 40
great hammerhead shark 11, 66, 72
Great Mayan Reef 85
great skua 220, 221
great white shark 7, 22, 52, 54, 56, 57, 59, 60, 62, 67, 75, 88, 97, 114–15, 116, 119, 120, 151
greater flamingo 217
green turtle 38–9, 209
Greenland shark 58, 134–5
ground sharks 53, 72, 73, 74–93
guitarfish 154–7
gulls 220, 221

habitats, damaged 26
half-naked hatchetfish 44
Halloween crab 239
hamerkops 218, 219
hammerhead shark 7, 11, 66, 72, 74–7
harbor porpoise 194–5
harbor seal 204–5
harlequin ghost pipefish 24–5
harlequin shrimp 240–1
hawksbill turtle 208, 209
Heermann's gull 221
hermit crabs 238
herons 218–19
herring gull 221
horn-eyed ghost crab 31
horn shark 146–7
horned boxfish 174–5
humpback whale 142, 188–9
humphead wrasse 26–7
hunting 24, 26, 48, 62
hydrothermal three-bearded rockling 47
hydrothermal vents 46–7

ice 29, 42
icefish 42
iguanas, marine 18, 19, 212–13
Indian Ocean 8, 9
Indonesian speckled shark 106–7
intertidal zone 30
invertebrates 14–15, 32, 36, 40, 41, 232–51

Japanese angelshark 152–3
Japanese bullhead shark 148–9
Japanese spider crab 239
jawless fish 12
jellyfish 234–5

Kamohoali'i 124
kelp forests 36–7
king penguin 231
kingdoms 10
kleptoparasitism 220, 221
krill 23, 94, 126

lanternsharks 136–7
Larids 220–1
lemon shark 65, 66, 86–7
lionfish 178–9

255

little gulper shark 48–9
little skate 166–7
lobsters 240–1
longfin mako shark 120
longnose sawshark 150–1

mackerel sharks 6, 73, 114–30
mako sharks 116–17, 119, 120
mammals 16–17, 42, 188–207
manatee 196–7
mandarin dragonet 181
mangrove forests 34–5, 87
mangrove pitta 35
manta ray 162
marine otter 201
marlin 182
Maui's dolphin 193
Megalodon 68–9
megamouth shark 126–7
melanophores 112
mermaid's purses 64
midnight zone 28, 44
mobula rays 162–3
mucus balloons 187
mudskippers 34
munk's devil ray 162–3
murres 33, 228, 229

narwhal 42–3, 190
necklace carpet shark 112–13
northern fur seal 206
nudibranchs 244–5
nurse shark 66–7, 100–1

oceanic whitetip 70–1
oceans 8–47
octopus 25, 236–7
oophagy 119
orangespot surgeonfish 176
ornate wobbegong 110–11
otters 200–1
oviparity 64
ovoviviparity 65, 141
oystercatchers 214

Pacific Islands 124
Pacific Ocean 8, 46, 47
Pacific seahorse 173
painted frogfish 185
panther torpedo ray 164–5
parakeet auklet 228
parasites 86, 103, 121, 134, 162
parrotfish 186–7
parthenogenesis 83
pearls 242
pelagic thresher 130–1
penguins 6, 230–1
petrels 222
photophores 45, 136, 143
phylums 14
phytoplankton 22, 126
pink shrimp 241
plovers 214–15
polar bears 198–9, 203
polar waters 42–3
polka dog stingray 160–1
polyps 7, 40, 232–3, 234
porbeagle 118–19, 120
porcupinefish 174
porpoises 190, 194–5
prawns 240
predators 24–5, 38, 41, 69
prey 24–5
producers 22, 23
puffadder shyshark 78–9
pufferfish 25, 174
puffins 228–9
purple-lined nudibranch 244–5
pursuit predators 24
pygmy shark 143
pygmy squid 233

rabbit fish 168–9
rays 154–67
red-footed booby 224
red knob starfish 246–7
red rock crab 238–9
reef stonefish 178
remoras 86, 162
reptiles 18–19, 208–13
requiem sharks 84–93
river stingrays 160–1
rocky shores 32–3
roseate spoonbill 218–19
rostrums 150, 151, 158, 159
rusty parrotfish 186–7

sailfish 182–3
salmon shark 119, 120–1
saltwater 8, 29
saltwater crocodile 22, 210–11
sand sharks 66
sand tiger shark 122–3
sanderling 31
sardines 63
sawfish 158–9
sawsharks 62, 73, 150–1, 158
scalloped hammerhead 74–5
scaly dragonfish 45
scorpionfish 178–9
Scoter ducks 226
sea anemones 232–3
sea cows 16, 196–7
sea cucumbers 248–9
sea lions 206
sea otters 200–1
sea pens 232, 233
sea slater 33
sea slugs and snails 244–5
sea snakes 18–19
sea turtles 18, 91, 208–9
sea urchins 25, 248–9
seadragons 173
seagrass meadows 38–9, 76
seahorses 172–3
seals 7, 198, 199, 204–7
sessile worms 250, 251
sharks 48–153, 154
    aggregations 66, 67, 129
    anatomy 52–3
    bites 53, 62, 63, 89, 116, 142, 146
    breathing 56–7, 104
    egg laying 64, 80, 148
    endangered and extinct 68–9, 70–1, 118, 122, 131, 138
    eyes 79, 90, 95, 98, 103, 105, 107, 111, 113, 115, 119, 121, 146
    feeding 62–3, 94, 126
    fins 52, 83
    freshwater 69, 89
    habitats 49
    human attacks 49, 63, 88, 92, 100, 111, 114
    hunting methods 62
    life cycle 64–5
    live pups 64, 65
    orders 72–3
    records 50, 51, 55, 56, 58, 116, 134, 141
    schools 66, 75
    scientific groups 73
    senses 60–1
    skeletons 50, 58
    skin 54–5, 139, 152
    sleeping 57
    species 72
    swimming 58–9, 77, 97
    teeth 52, 53, 76, 89, 91, 103, 114, 116, 117, 128, 137, 142, 149
    warm-blooded 120
    what a shark is 50–1
    see also individual species
shearwaters 222
shelduck, common 227
shoals 24, 245
short-quill sea pen 233

shortfin dwarf lionfish 179
shortfin mako shark 116–17, 120
shrimps 240, 241
shysharks 78–9
sixgill sawsharks 144
skates 166–7
skimmers 220
skuas 220, 221
slate pencil sea urchin 248–9
small-spotted catshark 66, 80–1
smalltooth sand tiger shark 124–5
snowy albatross 222, 223
sohal surgeonfish 177
southern bobtail squid 233
Southern Ocean 8, 42
southern right whale 189
southern rockhopper penguin 231
species 10, 11
spectacled eider 227
sperm whale 190–1
spinner dolphins 24
spiny dogfish 140–1
spiny lobster 240
spiracles 57, 79, 97, 107, 148, 156, 161, 165
spoonbills 218–19
squid 236–7
squirrelfish 13
starfish 246–7
starry dragonet 181
stilts 214, 215
stingrays 51, 160–1
striped dolphin 193
suction feeding 178
sunfish 13, 174, 175
sunstar, common 247
surgeonfish 7, 176–7
swell sharks 64–5
swim bladders 58
swordfish 182

tasselled wobbegong 108–9
temperature 28, 29
thresher sharks 130–1
tides 30
tiger shark 59, 88, 90–1, 92
toothed whales 190–5
tricolored heron 219
triggerfish 174
tubenoses 222–3
tuna 29, 117, 176
turbot 171
turtles, sea 18, 23, 38–9, 91, 208–9
tusks 202
twilight zone 28, 44

unicornfish 176, 177

vaquita porpoise 194
velvet belly lanternshark 136–7
viviparity 65

walrus 202–3
warty comb jelly 15
waves 9
western spiny brittle star 36
whale shark 50, 51, 55, 63, 67, 126, 94–5
whales 7, 26, 43, 188–95
whiskers 202
white marlin 183
white-tailed sea eagle 21
white whales 190
wide-eyed flounder 170–1
wobbegong sharks 54–5, 62, 108–11
worms 250–1
wrybill 214–15

yellow-lipped sea krait 19

zebra shark 96–7
zooplankton 22–3, 126, 128, 129, 163